Quick & Easy Recipes

PASTA *and* NOODLES

FOOD WRITERS' FAVORITES™

EDITED BY BARBARA GIBBS OSTMANN AND JANE L. BAKER

Food Writers' Favorites™ Series

Food Editors' Hometown Favorites
Food Editors' Favorites Treasured Recipes
Food Editors' Favorites Desserts
Food Writers' Favorites Soups, Stews and Casseroles
Food Writers' Favorites Cookies
Food Writers' Favorites Salads
Food Writers' Favorites Safe Party Planning: Beverages
Food Writers' Favorites Quick & Easy Recipes: Entrées
Food Writers' Favorites Safe Party Planning, Vol. 2
  Quick & Easy Recipes: Appetizers
Food Writers' Favorites Safe Party Planning, Vol. 3
  Quick & Easy Recipes: Grilling

Cover photography by Karen Meyers
Pasta drawings courtesy of The Pasta Association

Copyright 1996 © by Dial Publishing Company

ISBN 0-911479-14-7

Contents

About the Editors

Jane L. Baker is marketing director for the Cherry Marketing Institute in Michigan. She was food editor of *The Phoenix* (Ariz.) *Gazette* for 14 years. Jane uses her expertise as a home economist and writer to pursue free-lance writing and editing opportunities. She and Barbara are co-authors of *The Recipe Writers' Handbook,* a style manual.

Barbara Gibbs Ostmann writes about food and travel for The New York Times Regional Newspaper Group and other publications. She was food editor of the *St. Louis* (Mo.) *Post-Dispatch* for 16 years prior to becoming the coordinator of the Agricultural Journalism program at the University of Missouri-Columbia. She and Jane are co-authors of *The Recipe Writers' Handbook,* a style manual.

Contributing Writers

Jane L. Baker, East Lansing, MI; **Terry Briggs,** *The Macon Telegraph,* Macon, GA; **Toni Burks,** Roanoke, VA; **Narcisse S. Cadgène,** New York, NY; **Leona Carlson** (retired), *Rockford Register Star,* Rockford, IL; **Debra Carr-Elsing,** *The Capital Times,* Madison, WI; **Arlette Camp Copeland,** *The Macon Telegraph,* Macon, GA; **Dorothy Cunningham,** Morenci, MI; **Cynthia David,** *Toronto Sun,* Toronto, Ontario, Canada; **Beth Whitley Duke,** *Amarillo Globe-News,* Amarillo, TX; **Clara H. Eschmann,** *The Macon Telegraph,* Macon, GA; **Carolyn Flournoy,** *The Times,* Shreveport, LA; **Paula M. Galusha,** Tulsa, OK; **Janet Geissler,** *Lansing State Journal,* Lansing, MI; **Jane Gray,** Ludington Daily News, Ludington, MI; **Teri M. Grimes,** *The Bradenton Herald,* Bradenton, FL; **Lorrie Guttman,** *Tallahassee Democrat,* Tallahassee, FL; **Suzanne Hall,** *The Chattanooga Times,* Chattanooga, TN; **Delia A. Hammock,** *Good Housekeeping,* New York, NY; **Alice Handkins,** Wichita, KS; **Zack Hanle,** *Bon Appétit,* New York, NY; **Monetta L. Harr,** *Jackson Citizen Patriot,* Jackson, MI; **Ann Hattes,** Hartland, WI; **Constance Hay,** Columbia, MD; **Jim Hillibish,** *The Repository,* Canton, OH; **Susan Manlin Katzman,** St. Louis, MO; **Stacy Lam,** *The Macon Telegraph,* Macon, GA; **Lori Longbotham,** New York, NY; **Janice Okun,** *Buffalo News,* Buffalo, NY; **Beth W. Orenstein,** Northhampton, PA; **Eleanor Ostman,** *St. Paul Pioneer Press,* St. Paul, MN; **Barbara Gibbs Ostmann,** St. Louis, MO; **Christine W. Randall,** *The Post and Courier,* Charleston, SC; **Sally L. Scherer,** *The Macon Telegraph,* Macon, GA; **Mary D. Scourtes,** *The Tampa Tribune,* Tampa, FL; **Kathleen Desmond Stang,** Seattle, WA; **Anita Stewart,** Elora, Ontario, Canada; **Caroline Stuart,** Greenwich, CT; **Jeanne Voltz,** Pittsboro, NC; **Julie Watson,** Charlottetown, Prince Edward Island, Canada; **Kasey Wilson,** *The Vancouver Courier,* Vancouver, British Columbia, Canada; **Barbara Yost,** *The Phoenix Gazette,* Phoenix, AZ.

Before you start cooking

Perhaps no other type of food is more appropriate for so many different types of occasions than pasta.

Whether you are planning an intimate dinner for two or a gala celebration for two hundred, pasta is a versatile and delicious addition to nearly any meal.

Easy to prepare and wonderfully satisfying, pasta can be served as appetizers, entrees, and even desserts. In fact, you can create an entire dinner consisting of all pasta dishes.

Mothers Against Drunk Driving (MADD) is pleased to present this special pasta edition of the *Food Writers' Favorites™/Quick & Easy Recipes.* We are certain that your family and friends will enjoy preparing, serving, and, of course, eating the wonderful recipes on the following pages for many years to come.

We urge you to never let a dinner or party companion drive after drinking. And please remember never to serve alcohol to anyone under the age of 21. And every bit as important, please make a personal pledge to never drive under the influence of alcohol. Keep in mind that even one alcoholic drink can seriously affect a person's ability to drive safely.

Before you sample the delightful pasta recipes in this edition of *Food Writers' Favorites™,* please take a few moments to read the rest of this section. The following pages will help you learn more about MADD and what you can do to help us reduce the threat of alcohol-impaired driving on our nation's streets and highways.

Mothers Against Drunk Driving

The mission of Mothers Against Drunk Driving is to stop drunk driving and to support victims of this violent crime.

We're still MADD

Mothers Against Drunk Driving was founded in 1980 after a California woman's daughter was killed by a hit-and-run driver. Incredibly, the driver had been released from jail on bail just two days earlier — for another drunk driving hit-and-run crime.

Determined to stop the tragic loss of life caused by drinking and driving, the girl's mother and others in her community formed the first chapter of MADD.

Today, that one small group of committed women has grown to a nationwide movement with more than 500 community action teams, chapters and state organizations.

And MADD is not just for mothers. Our members and supporters include fathers, sons, brothers, grandparents and uncles. In fact, anyone can join MADD. The only requirement is a commitment to end alcohol and other drug-impaired driving.

Since MADD began, more than 2,000 anti-drunk driving laws have been passed nationwide. These laws are helping police, prosecutors and judges remove impaired drivers from our highways — and keep them off.

But laws alone can't stop people from drinking and driving.

MADD is educating the public about the dangers of impaired driving. Through programs like Designated Driver and Project Red Ribbon, we're spreading this important message across America — drinking and driving must stop.

After more than a decade of battling drinking and driving, we're still MADD. And we're still committed to ending the senseless injuries and deaths caused by drunk driving and to providing assistance to the many victims of this senseless and preventable crime.

You can help MADD
MADD needs your help — because drinking and driving affects everyone.

Along with the human toll in destroyed lives, drunk driving costs the United States $44 billion every year in direct expenses. An additional $90 billion is lost in quality of life due to these crashes.

As a team, MADD and you are working to keep drunk drivers off our highways. Here are a few ways you can make a difference:

• Make a personal promise to never drink and drive.

• Don't let friends or relatives drive under the influence of alcohol or other drugs.

• Speak out in your community against alcohol and other drug-impaired driving.

• Support tougher legislation against drunk driving. Tell your local, county, state, and federal representatives that their help is needed to end drinking and driving.

• Use a Designated Driver if you drink when you're out. Encourage friends and relatives to use and to be Designated Drivers.

• Warn the young people in your life about the dangers of under-age drinking and impaired driving.

• Never serve alcohol to anyone under 21 years old or anyone who has had too much to drink.

• Report impaired drivers to the police.

• Remember that a person's ability to drive can be greatly affected by alcohol long before he or she appears to be intoxicated.

Your help makes a difference
Thanks to the help of millions of concerned and committed people across America, alcohol-related traffic deaths have decreased about 40% percent since MADD was founded in 1980.

But there's so much more hard work ahead of us.

Two out of every five Americans will be involved in an alcohol- or other drug-related crash during their lives. We want to reduce those odds—and protect you from the threat of drinking and driving.

In 1994, an estimated 16,589 people died and 297,000 people were injured as the result of alcohol-related crashes on the nation's highways.

Each death and injury is a solemn reminder that MADD must continue the battle against drinking and driving. And we will continue to do everything possible to make our roads safer — for everyone.

MADD's goals

In 1990, MADD released its "20 By 2000" plan – to reduce the proportion of traffic fatalities which were alcohol-related from 50% to 40% by the year 2000. Since that time this proportion dropped from 50% to 40.8% in 1994. We have nearly reached our goal, but there's still much to do. The "20 By 2000" plan includes:

- *Youth Issues*
  Education, prevention and penalties for alcohol and other drug use by those under age 21, whether driving or not.

- *Enforcement*
  Sobriety checkpoints, a .08 blood alcohol content limit and mandatory testing of drivers involved in fatal and serious injury crashes.

- *Sanctions*
  Administrative license revocation, plate or vehicle confiscation for repeat offenders and equal penalties for death and serious injury DUI/DWI offenses.

- *Self-Sufficiency*
  DUI/DWI fines, fees, and other assessments to fund programs to prevent, detect and deter impaired driving.

- *Responsible Marketing & Service of Alcohol*
  Uniform closing hours for drinking establishments, Designated Driver programs, server training and an end to happy hours.

- *Amendments for Victims Rights*
  State constitutional amendments to ensure that victims will be informed of, present at and heard in the criminal justice process.

- *Compensation for Victims*
  Restitution and victim compensation programs to ensure adequate financial recovery for victims.

- *Dram Shop Recovery*
  Legislation or case law to allow victims the right to seek financial recovery from servers who provide alcohol to those who are intoxicated or to minors who then cause fatal or serious injury crashes.

- *Endangerment of Children*
  Legislation to enhance the sanctions of convicted impaired drivers who drive with a minor child in the vehicle.

MADD is on your side

Mothers Against Drunk Driving is more committed than ever to protecting you, your family and your friends from the threat of alcohol- and other drug-related driving crashes.

But we want you to know that MADD is only a phone call away if you or anyone you know is ever the victim of a drunk driving crash.

Call our hot line at 1-800-GET-MADD. Our trained staff is prepared to give victims emotional support and information about the criminal justice system. And we'll direct victims to the MADD chapter nearest them, so that they can receive the personalized support they need.

MADD can help stop the alcohol- and other drug-related crashes that destroy so many lives each year. Please, help us in whatever way you can to make our highways safer. Thank you.

If you would like more information on MADD in your local community or how to get more involved, write: MADD National Office, 511 E. John Carpenter Freeway, Suite 700, Irving, TX 75062 *or call:* 1-800-GET-MADD

Pasta *and* Noodles

Everyone loves pasta. It's quick and easy to prepare, packed with nutrients and combines deliciously with almost any food.

The popularity of pasta certainly is evident in the recipes contributed by food editors and writers for this cookbook. They shared their tried-and-true personal favorites as well as many regional specialties.

Of the hundreds of recipes submitted for this book, by far the most popular was some version of macaroni and cheese. Repeatedly editors said macaroni and cheese was their comfort food, from childhood through adulthood. We created a special chapter to highlight some of the best versions of this classic dish.

There's also a chapter that features a mouth-watering collection of unusual pastas, such as gnocchi, couscous and dumplings. The dozens of recipes in the book range from savory to sweet — that's right, some of the pasta recipes are appropriate for dessert.

You'll also find information about various pasta shapes and tips on cooking with pasta. For those of you who enjoy reading cookbooks, each recipe includes a brief introduction that tells you something about the recipe.

We would like to make it clear that these recipes are the contributors' favorites. The publisher makes no claim that the recipes are original. When possible, credit has been given where credit is due.

We hope the recipes in this book will help you to discover a new world of pasta-bilities. Enjoy!

Jane L. Baker and Barbara Gibbs Ostmann
Editors of *Food Writers' Favorites*™
Quick & Easy Recipes: Pasta and Noodles

Pasta Parade

Pasta comes in many shapes and sizes. Changing the pasta shape can make a big difference in the taste and flavor of the recipe. As a general rule, thin, delicate pasta, such as angel hair or thin spaghetti, should be served with light, thin sauces. Thicker pasta shapes, such as fettuccine, work well with heavier sauces. Pasta shapes with holes or ridges, such as mostaccioli or spirals, are perfect for chunkier sauces. Experimenting with various pasta shapes is part of the fun of cooking with pasta.

Here is a description of some of the basic shapes and how they might best be used. Sometimes a particular shape has more than one name. The English translation of the Italian word (shown here in parenthesis) often is helpful in remembering the name of a particular shape.

Angel hair or capellini *(fine hairs)*: This pasta usually is used in soups or with light, delicate sauces; it's often sold coiled.

Bow tie pasta or farfalle *(butterflies)*: These come in small, medium and large sizes. They are thick enough for most sauces and are excellent in salads or soups.

Cannelloni *(large reeds)*: These large pasta tubes, or squares of pasta that have been rolled into tubes, usually are cooked and stuffed, then topped with sauce and baked.

Ditali *(thimbles)* **or ditalini** *(little thimbles)*: These short lengths of pasta are versatile. They can be baked or used in soups or salads.

Egg noodles *(from the German word nudel, meaning pasta with egg)*: There are various widths of egg noodles, which can be used to create soups, salads and casseroles or topped with almost any sauce. Cholesterol-free and eggless noodles are available.

 Elbow macaroni *(dumpling)*: These are short, curved tubes of pasta that are available in many colors and sizes. Macaroni holds up well in baked pasta recipes.

 Fusilli *(little springs)*: Long strands of spaghetti-size pasta that appear to have been twisted on a spindle. They can be used in place of spaghetti. Some pasta manufacturers use the name fusilli for rotelle (see listing).

Fettuccine *(small ribbons)*: This long, thick pasta is perfect for heavier sauces, such as cheese, meat and tomato sauces.

 Gnocchi *(lumps)*: Homemade gnocchi, which look like dumplings, can be made with mashed potatoes, cornmeal, ricotta cheese or semolina. A number of pasta manufacturers make a dried gnocchi that can be used like medium-size macaroni.

 Lasagna *(from the Latin word lasanum, which means pot)*: These are wide ribbons of pasta, sometimes with curly edges, sometimes with straight edges, that most often are used in baked recipes. The size varies from 1- to $2\frac{1}{2}$-inches wide.

 Linguine *(little tongues)*: This is an oval-shaped pasta that is halfway between a flat ribbon and a cylindrical strand. It's a great shape for all sauces as well as a good choice for salads and stir-fry recipes.

 Macaroni: This is the U.S. pasta industry's generic term for any dried wheat product. However, in most recipes macaroni means dried pasta tubes of assorted sizes, such as elbow macaroni.

 Manicotti *(little muffs)*: One of the larger tubes of pasta, it's available ridged or smooth. It is usually cooked and stuffed, then covered with sauce and baked.

Mostaccioli *(small mustaches)*: This is a tubular pasta, about 2- inches long with a ridged or smooth exterior and diagonally cut ends. It's especially good with a chunky meat sauce or robust tomato sauce, but also is used in salads and baked in casseroles. Sometimes mostaccioli is called penne (quills).

Orzo: This small, grain-shaped pasta can be topped with any sauce, added to soups or baked in a casserole. It is often used as a side dish or as a salad.

Pastina: This tiny pasta is often used in soups or broths.

Penne: See Mostaccioli.

Ravioli: A square, stuffed pasta, it's usually served with a sauce or in a soup.

Rigatoni: Large, 1 1/2- inch long tubes with ridges. It's particularly good with spicy sauces as well as cream and cheese sauces.

Rotelle *(little wheels)*: These are small, spoked-wheel shapes that are great with chunky sauces.

Rotini: The twisted shape of this pasta holds bits of meat, vegetables and cheese, so it works well with almost any sauce. Rotini is often used in salads; it also holds its shape well in baked recipes.

Shells: There are several sizes of this pasta. Small or medium shells are used in soups and salads and often replace traditional elbow macaroni in macaroni and cheese recipes. Jumbo shells are most often stuffed with a mixture of cheese, meat or vegetables.

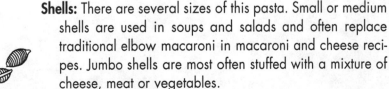

Spaghetti *(little strands)*: This is the best known pasta. It comes in many sizes, from very fine to fairly thick. Although spaghetti is traditionally served with a tomato sauce, it's also a good choice for many other kinds of sauces and can be used in casseroles and stir-fry recipes.

Tagliatelle: These cut noodles are interchangeable with fettuccine. Tagliarini are narrow tagliatelle.

Tortellini *(little twists)*: Filled like ravioli but with a different shape, this pasta is often used in soups and sometimes served with a sauce.

Vermicelli *(little worms)*: These fine strands of spaghetti are slightly thicker than angel hair pasta. Vermicelli can be purchased straight or in coils.

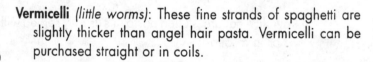

Ziti *(bridegrooms)*: A medium-size, tubular pasta shape, it's perfect for chunky sauces and meat dishes. It's similar to mostaccioli.

Pasta Pointers

When cooking with pasta, keep these tips in mind:

- It's best to cook pasta according to the specific instructions on the pasta package. However, the general instructions for cooking perfect pasta is to use 4 to 6 quarts of water for each pound of pasta. Bring water to boiling. Add pasta; stir and return to boiling. Stir the pasta occasionally during cooking. Use the time on the package as a guide, but taste the pasta to determine if it is done. Perfectly cooked pasta should be *al dente,* or firm to the bite yet cooked through. Fresh homemade pasta and store-bought refrigerated pasta products cook more quickly than dried pasta.

- If using cooked pasta in a baked recipe, undercook it slightly because it will continue to cook and absorb liquid during baking.

- Unsalted water will come to boiling faster than salted water, so if you want to add salt to the cooking liquid, do so after it comes to boiling.

- Adding a small amount of vegetable oil to the cooking water keeps it from boiling over the pot and keeps the pasta from sticking together while cooking.

- Uncooked dried pasta can be stored in the cupboard for up to one year in an airtight container. Dried whole wheat pasta is the exception. It can turn rancid if stored at room temperature longer than one month. Store it in the refrigerator.

- Homemade pasta is best used immediately. It can be stored in the refrigerator for a day or two in an airtight container. It's also possible to dry homemade pasta although it is quite fragile and breaks easily. Once it is dried, store it in airtight containers.

- The best pasta shapes for freezing are those that are used in baked recipes, such as lasagna, jumbo shells, ziti or manicotti. You'll have better results if you prepare the recipe and freeze it before baking. To bake, let the dish thaw to room temperature, then bake as the recipe directs.

- Cooked pasta can be refrigerated in an airtight container for 3 to 5 days. However, because cooked pasta continues to absorb flavors and oils from sauces, store cooked pasta separately from the sauce.

- Pasta can be cooked in advance. Drain, then toss with a teaspoon of vegetable oil. Refrigerate in an airtight container. Reheat in a microwave oven on High (100% power) 45 seconds at a time, stirring between heatings. Or you can reheat cooked pasta by immersing it in a pot of boiling water for one to two minutes.

- Spaghetti and macaroni products generally double in volume after cooking, while egg noodles don't expand as much. One pound of dried macaroni-type pasta equals about 4 cups uncooked, 8 cups cooked. One pound dried spaghetti-type pasta is about 4 cups uncooked, 7 to 8 cups cooked. One pound of egg noodles is about 10 cups uncooked, 12 cups cooked.

- Generally you will need about 2 ounces of dried pasta to make a side-dish serving and 4 ounces for a main-course serving.

- Pasta not only tastes good, but it's also good for you. Two ounces of dried pasta contains no cholesterol, no sodium, only 210 calories and less than one gram of fat.

Vegetables *and* Herbs

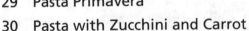

Asparagus Pasta

Narcisse S. Cadgène
Free-Lance Writer, New York, NY

This is probably my all-time favorite springtime pasta dish. It's light as a feather, but with plenty of flavor. If someone in the family isn't an anchovy fan, make this anyway. The anchovies lend body and piquancy as they do in a Caesar salad, but in the same way as in the Caesar dressing, the fishy flavor doesn't come through.

Makes 4 servings

2 pounds fresh asparagus
1/4 cup Dijon-style mustard
1/4 cup olive oil
6 anchovy fillets
2 cloves garlic, quartered

2/3 cup quartered shallots
1/2 teaspoon dried thyme
16 ounces thin spaghetti
1/4 cup chopped fresh parsley
Salt and freshly ground
    black pepper

Trim tough white ends of asparagus; cut asparagus into 1/2-inch lengths, leaving the tips intact. Meanwhile, bring a large saucepan of unsalted water to boiling. Drop asparagus into water; simmer 4 to 5 minutes, or until just tender. Drain; rinse briefly with cool water to stop the cooking. Drain well; set aside.

Combine mustard, olive oil and anchovy fillets in container of electric blender or food processor; blend or process until anchovies are pureed. Add garlic; pulse 3 to 4 times, or until garlic is just chunky. Add shallots and thyme; pulse 3 to 4 times, or until shallots are chopped but not pureed.

Cook spaghetti al dente, according to package directions. Drain, reserving 1 cup cooking liquid. Add 1/2 cup of the reserved cooking liquid to anchovy mixture in blender. Pulse 1 to 2 times to combine.

Combine drained pasta, reserved asparagus and parsley; toss to mix. Pour anchovy sauce over pasta mixture; add some of the remaining cooking liquid if mixture seems too dry. Season to taste with salt and pepper. Serve immediately.

Broccoli Lasagna

Janet Geissler
Food Editor, *Lansing State Journal*, Lansing, MI

Are you trying to cut down on meat? You will never miss it in this vegetable lasagna. This recipe is a twist on the typical vegetarian lasagna, which is usually made with zucchini or spinach.

Makes 12 servings

2 (10 3/4-ounce) cans cream of broccoli soup, undiluted
1 (10-ounce) package frozen chopped broccoli, thawed
4 tablespoons vegetable oil, divided
2 carrots, thinly sliced
1 large onion, finely chopped
1/4 cup water
3/4 pound fresh mushrooms, sliced
12 lasagna noodles
2 (8-ounce) packages shredded mozzarella cheese
1 (15-ounce) carton ricotta cheese
2 eggs

Combine soup and broccoli in a medium saucepan; cook, stirring occasionally, until warm.

Heat 1 tablespoon of the oil in a 10-inch skillet over medium-high heat. Add carrots and onion; cook, stirring, until light brown. Reduce heat to low; stir in water. Simmer, covered, 15 minutes, or until vegetables are quite tender. Transfer carrot mixture to a bowl; reserve.

In the same skillet, heat remaining 3 tablespoons oil over high heat. Add mushrooms; cook, stirring, until light brown and liquid has evaporated. Add reserved carrot mixture; stir to combine.

Meanwhile, cook lasagna noodles according to package directions. Drain well. In a medium bowl, combine mozzarella cheese, ricotta cheese and eggs; mix well.

To assemble lasagna, spread 1 cup broccoli sauce in a 13x9x2-inch baking pan. Arrange 6 cooked noodles on sauce. Top with half of the cheese mixture, all of the carrot mixture, and half of the remaining broccoli sauce. Top with remaining 6 cooked noodles, remaining cheese mixture and remaining broccoli sauce. Bake in a preheated 375° oven 45 minutes. Remove from oven; let stand 10 minutes before cutting and serving.

Easy Ramen Supper

Christine W. Randall
Assistant Features Editor, *The Post and Courier*, Charleston, SC

For some reason, it took me a long time to discover ramen noodles. But when I did, I took to them in a big way. I buy them at a discount supermarket in a box of 24 so I always have them on hand, whether I want a simple cup of soup or a potluck entree. This is a great recipe for using whatever you might have in your refrigerator or freezer. I find that frozen vegetables work as well as fresh.

Makes 4 servings

3 tablespoons olive oil
4 cups chopped vegetables
   (broccoli, snow peas, carrots,
   onion, corn or whatever
   you have on hand)

2 (3-ounce) packages instant
   ramen noodles (any flavor)
1 2/3 cups water

Heat olive oil in large skillet or wok. Add vegetables; cook, stirring over high heat, 1 minute. Coarsely crumble dry noodles. Stir in noodles, noodle seasoning packets and water. Cover and steam 3 to 5 minutes, or until liquid is absorbed, stirring twice during cooking time. Serve immediately.

Note: If desired, cut-up cooked meat (such as smoked sausage) can be substituted for some of the vegetables. Recipe can be halved.

Remember: all forms of alcoholic beverages are drugs.

Fettuccine Florentine

Paula M. Galusha
Free-Lance Home Economist, Tulsa, OK

In Oklahoma, pecans are a prized crop. My brother-in-law, J. Harley Galusha, had a large pecan orchard about 45 minutes from Tulsa. Harvesting the pecans in the fall became a traditional family outing. We would go early in the morning and take a picnic lunch. It was a real education to watch the machines shake pecans from the trees, gather them, and take them to the barn, where they were sorted and cracked by more machines. For me, creating recipes using these luscious pecans became part of the tradition.

Makes 4 servings

1 1/2 cups half-and-half or light cream, divided	1/8 teaspoon hot pepper sauce
2/3 cup pecan pieces, divided	8 ounces spinach fettuccine
3 tablespoons butter or margarine	1/4 pound prosciutto or smoked ham, cut into thin strips
1 teaspoon dried sage	1/4 cup chopped fresh parsley

In container of electric blender, combine 1/2 cup of the half-and-half and 1/3 cup of the pecans. Blend until almost smooth. Pour mixture into a medium saucepan. Add the remaining 1 cup half-and-half, butter, sage and hot pepper sauce. Bring just to boiling, stirring occasionally; reduce heat and simmer 2 minutes.

Meanwhile, cook fettuccine according to package directions. Drain well.

Put fettuccine and prosciutto in a large serving dish. Pour cream sauce over pasta mixture; mix gently. Sprinkle parsley and remaining 1/3 cup pecans over all. Serve immediately.

Hasta La Pasta

Beth Whitley Duke
Food Editor, *Amarillo Globe-News*, Amarillo, TX

In Spanish, "hasta" means later. "Hasta la vista" is a common expression among friends who don't want to say good-bye; it means simply, "See you later." I call this dish Hasta La Pasta because it brings to mind an easy supper to mark the end of a busy day. This is a good recipe to keep handy for when you want to celebrate the fresh zucchini, tomatoes and peppers in your summer garden.

Makes 4 servings

2 tablespoons vegetable oil
1 medium onion, sliced
3 cloves garlic, finely chopped
2 medium zucchini, sliced
2 medium tomatoes, cut into wedges
2 poblano peppers, sliced (see note)
1 cup fresh or frozen whole-kernel corn
2 tablespoons chili powder

1 teaspoon dried oregano
1/2 teaspoon ground cumin
2 tablespoons finely chopped fresh cilantro or parsley
1/2 teaspoon salt
1/4 teaspoon black pepper
8 ounces trio maliano pasta (a combination of spiral pasta, shell macaroni and rigatoni; about 2 cups total)

Heat oil in a large skillet. Add onion and garlic; cook, stirring, about 5 minutes, or until onion is tender. Add zucchini, tomatoes, poblano peppers, corn, chili powder, oregano and cumin; mix well. Cook, uncovered, over medium heat 12 to 15 minutes, stirring occasionally, or until vegetables are crisp-tender. Remove from heat. Stir in cilantro, salt and pepper.

Meanwhile, cook pasta according to package directions. Drain well.

Spoon vegetable mixture over hot pasta; mix gently. Serve immediately.

Note: If poblano peppers are not available, substitute 2 green bell peppers, and add one jalapeño, finely chopped, to the onions as they cook.

Even one drink can affect a person's ability to drive safely.

Hearty Vegetable Fettuccine

Alice Handkins
Free-Lance Food Writer, Wichita, KS

Start with tri-color fettuccine, add lots of stir-fried vegetables, and you have a delicious one-dish meal that can be prepared in about 10 minutes. I like using tri-color fettuccine, but this tastes just as good with spaghetti, rotini or other pasta. The vegetables I most frequently use are specified in the recipe, but you can use the vegetables your family prefers. Celery, yellow squash, green bell peppers and cauliflower work well.

Makes 4 servings

2 tablespoons vegetable oil	1 (8-ounce) can tomato sauce
1 medium onion, sliced into strips	1/2 teaspoon salt
2 cloves garlic, finely chopped	1/2 teaspoon Italian seasoning
1 medium zucchini, sliced	1/4 teaspoon black pepper
8 ounces fresh mushrooms, sliced	8 ounces tri-color fettuccine
2 large tomatoes, cubed	Freshly grated Parmesan cheese

Heat oil in a large skillet. Add onion and garlic; cook, stirring, 1 minute. Add zucchini and mushrooms; cook, stirring constantly, 2 to 3 minutes, or until mushrooms start to look cooked. Add tomatoes; cook 2 to 3 minutes. Add tomato sauce, salt, Italian herbs and pepper; mix well. Cook, stirring, over medium heat until vegetable mixture is hot. Taste and adjust seasonings, if necessary.

Meanwhile, cook fettuccine according to package directions. Drain well. Put cooked pasta in a large bowl; pour vegetable sauce over pasta. Serve immediately. Pass Parmesan cheese at the table.

Hearty Vegetarian Pasta Sauce

Constance Hay
Free-Lance Food Writer, Columbia, MD

Because more and more people are vegetarians, it is essential to have a good recipe for vegetable pasta sauce on hand. Actually, I think anyone can appreciate this hearty sauce – your guests will never miss the meat. Although any type of fresh mushroom can be used, it is fun to experiment with the exotic varieties, such as crimini or shiitake, which have a meaty flavor. If you are not vegetarian and don't have vegetable broth on hand, substitute beef broth.

Makes 4 cups sauce; enough for 4 servings of pasta

2 tablespoons olive oil, divided
8 ounces crimini or other fresh
   mushrooms, thinly sliced
2 zucchini, shredded
1 onion, chopped
1 red bell pepper, thinly sliced
1 (15-ounce) can tomato purée

1/2 cup vegetable broth
1 teaspoon Italian seasoning
1 teaspoon granulated sugar
1/2 teaspoon garlic salt
1/4 teaspoon black pepper
8 ounces spaghetti or other pasta

Heat 1 tablespoon of the oil in a large skillet over medium-high heat. Add mushrooms; cook, stirring constantly, 2 to 3 minutes, or until mushrooms are tender. Remove mushrooms from skillet; reserve.

Heat remaining 1 tablespoon oil in same skillet. Add zucchini, onion and bell pepper; cook, stirring occasionally, 5 to 7 minutes, or until vegetables are tender. Stir in tomato purée, vegetable broth, Italian seasoning, sugar, garlic salt, pepper and reserved mushrooms. Simmer 15 to 20 minutes. If necessary, add additional broth for proper consistency.

Meanwhile, cook pasta according to package directions. Drain well. Serve hot sauce over cooked pasta.

Cold showers, coffee, or fresh air won't sober up a drunk — only time will help.

Instant Pasta Chinoise

Zack Hanle
Editor-at-Large, *Bon Appétit*, New York, NY

This recipe was concocted for a favorite grandson who enjoyed cooking Chinese dishes but who didn't have enough time at college to chop and slice lots of vegetables. The whole dish takes about as much time as is needed to cook and drain the pasta.

Makes 2 servings

6 ounces spinach or plain fettuccine
2 tablespoons peanut oil or
    vegetable oil
1 (10-ounce) package frozen
    mixed vegetables, thawed

2 cloves garlic, finely chopped
1 tablespoon soy sauce

Cook fettuccine according to package directions. Drain well.

Meanwhile, heat oil in a wok or skillet. Add vegetables; cook, stirring, 2 to 3 minutes. Stir in garlic and soy sauce. Cook until vegetables are just tender.

Put pasta into 2 pasta bowls or large serving plates. Top each with half of the vegetables. Serve immediately.

Orzo with Tomatoes and Pine Nuts

Caroline Stuart
Cookbook Author, Greenwich, CT

Orzo is a small rice-shaped pasta that is sold alongside other dried pasta in supermarkets. Although it is often overlooked by cooks, orzo is absolutely delicious in soups, salads or almost any dish that calls for rice. It also works well in vegetable side dishes. Try orzo stuffed in tomato or zucchini shells, or even corn husks. Include this orzo dish on your next picnic or as a side dish at your next dinner party. I haven't met anyone yet who doesn't like it.

Makes 4 to 6 servings

2 tablespoons olive oil or
   vegetable oil
¼ cup pine nuts
2 tablespoons sliced green onions
4 medium tomatoes, chopped
3 tablespoons finely chopped
   fresh parsley

4 ounces orzo (1 cup)
2 tablespoons grated
   Parmesan cheese
Salt and freshly ground
   black pepper

Heat oil in a medium saucepan over low heat. Add pine nuts; cook, stirring, a few minutes, or until nuts are light brown. Remove nuts from oil with a slotted spoon; place on paper towels to drain.

Add green onions and tomatoes to oil in pan; cook, stirring, over medium-low heat until tomatoes are softened but still firm. Stir in parsley. Keep tomato sauce warm over low heat.

Meanwhile, cook orzo according to package directions. Drain well. Return orzo to cooking pot. Add tomato sauce and Parmesan cheese; mix well. Season to taste with salt and pepper.

Spoon into a serving bowl; sprinkle pine nuts on top. Serve immediately.

It's a fact: alcohol is a drug.

Pasta Con Broccoli

Susan Manlin Katzman
Free-Lance Food Writer, St. Louis, MO

This is my family's favorite pasta recipe. I've made it over and over through the years, because it is always requested for birthdays and other family party dinners. The ingredients are adjustable; add more or less butter, cream or cheese and the recipe still works. You can even change the vegetables. For example, use half broccoli and half cauliflower and substitute spinach noodles for shell macaroni.

Makes 6 to 8 servings

1 bunch broccoli (about 1 pound)
10 ounces shell macaroni or
    similar pasta (4 cups)
About 3 tablespoons butter

About 3/4 cup heavy cream
About 2/3 cup grated
    Parmesan cheese
Salt, to taste

Trim leaves and coarse stems from broccoli. Cut tender stems and tops into bite-size pieces.

In a large pot, bring at least 5 quarts water to boiling. Add pasta; boil 3 minutes. Add broccoli pieces; boil about 7 minutes, or until pasta and broccoli are just tender. Drain well.

Put pasta and broccoli in a large serving bowl. Add butter and cream; toss with 2 large spoons until butter melts and most of the cream soaks into pasta. Add cheese; mix gently. Season with salt and, if desired, add more butter, cream or cheese. Serve immediately.

Pasta Picante

Jane Gray
Food Editor, *Ludington Daily News*, Ludington, MI

While planning recipes for a food page devoted to eating more healthfully, I came across this recipe from the American Institute for Cancer Research. It's a basic pasta and tomato dish, but it has a hearty flavor that eliminates the need for meat. However, it's versatile enough that you can add meat or other ingredients to the recipe according to your own taste.

Makes 4 servings

2 tablespoons olive oil
3 cloves garlic, finely chopped
1 medium onion, chopped
1 large zucchini, cubed
1/2 green or red bell pepper, chopped
1 (10-ounce) can tomatoes and green chilies (with or without cilantro), drained

1/2 cup chopped fresh basil or 1 tablespoon dried
1/2 cup chopped fresh parsley
12 ounces fettuccine
1/4 cup grated Parmesan cheese

Heat oil in a large skillet. Add garlic and onion; cook, stirring, until onion is translucent. Add zucchini and bell pepper; cook, stirring, over medium-high heat 2 minutes, or until tender-crisp. Add tomatoes, basil and parsley. Cook, stirring frequently, until heated through.

Meanwhile, cook fettuccine according to package directions. Drain well. Put fettuccine in a warmed serving bowl. Add vegetable sauce; mix gently. Sprinkle Parmesan cheese on top. Serve immediately.

It is time to treat drunk driving as a serious crime.

Pasta Primavera

Kathleen Desmond Stang
Free-Lance Food Writer, Seattle, WA

I make this pretty, pink-and-green spring dish with fresh asparagus and leftover baked ham jazzed up with the homemade pesto I keep in my freezer. When asparagus is out of season, substitute sliced zucchini or another vegetable. Do all the chopping first; you should have about 3 cups of vegetables total.

Makes 2 or 3 servings

1 teaspoon olive oil
1 cup diagonally sliced asparagus
1/2 cup sliced onion
  (1 small onion)
1 cup sliced fresh mushrooms
  (about 4 mushrooms)
3/4 cup diced cooked ham
1/2 cup frozen peas, thawed
1/4 cup chicken or vegetable broth

1/4 cup light sour cream
About 2 tablespoons pesto
  (homemade or store-bought)
1 tablespoon finely chopped fresh
  parsley (preferably flat leaf)
Salt and black pepper, to taste
6 ounces linguine or other pasta
Grated Parmesan cheese (optional)

Heat oil in a large nonstick skillet over medium-high heat. Add asparagus and onion; cook, stirring, 2 minutes. Add mushrooms; cook, stirring, 1 to 2 minutes. Stir in ham and peas; cook, stirring, 1 minute, or until vegetables are tender-crisp. Add broth, sour cream, pesto, parsley, salt and pepper; mix well. Cook and stir until thoroughly heated.

Meanwhile, cook linguine according to package directions. Drain well.

Put linguine in a warmed serving dish. Spoon sauce over pasta. Sprinkle Parmesan cheese on top, if desired. Serve immediately.

Pasta with Zucchini and Carrot

Suzanne Hall
Food Editor, *The Chattanooga Times*, Chattanooga, TN

Associated with Chattanooga's Heart Institute, the Healthy Heart Cafe originally was established to serve out-patients and visitors to the institute and nearby hospitals. Its good food, however, soon made it a popular lunch spot for anyone in the area. Registered dietitians design the menus and recipes to be healthful and delicious, as in this colorful pasta recipe. If yellow bell pepper is unavailable or too expensive, substitute a green or red bell pepper.

Makes 6 servings

2 tablespoons margarine
2 cloves garlic, finely chopped
1 carrot, cut into julienne strips
1 zucchini, cut into julienne strips
1 yellow bell pepper, cut into
   julienne strips

4 ounces fettuccine
1/4 cup finely chopped
   fresh parsley
1/4 cup grated Parmesan cheese
1/8 teaspoon freshly ground
   black pepper

Melt margarine in a large skillet over medium heat. Add garlic and carrot; cook, stirring, 5 minutes. Add zucchini, bell pepper and enough water to prevent sticking (1 to 2 tablespoons); cook, stirring, 3 minutes.

Meanwhile, cook pasta according to package directions. Drain well. Put pasta in a warmed serving bowl. Add cooked vegetables, parsley, Parmesan cheese and pepper; mix gently. Serve immediately.

Ask what police, judges and lawmakers are doing to end drunk driving.

Peppers with Pasta and Mushrooms

Clara H. Eschmann
Food Columnist, *The Macon Telegraph*, Macon, GA

I created this recipe out of necessity. I had purchased too many red, yellow and green bell peppers. Because they were expensive, I didn't want to waste them, so I cut them into julienne strips and combined them with pasta. It turned out to be a good recipe, and I use it often to add zip and color to my menus.

Makes 4 to 6 servings

3 tablespoons olive oil
3 bell peppers (red, yellow or green), cut into julienne strips
1 cup sliced fresh mushrooms

1 tablespoon finely chopped onion
Salt and black pepper
4 ounces shell macaroni (1 1/2 cups)

Heat oil in skillet. Add bell peppers, mushrooms and onion. Cook, stirring, until vegetables are tender. Season to taste with salt and pepper.

Meanwhile, cook pasta according to package directions. Drain well.

Combine pasta and cooked vegetables; mix gently. Serve immediately.

Puglia-Style Pasta

Barbara Gibbs Ostmann
Food Writer, St. Louis, MO

Puglia (also called Apulia) is a little-known area of southern Italy, right in the heel of the boot. It is a delightful area to visit because you won't find hordes of tourists. What you will find is a beautiful countryside dotted with unusual beehive-shaped houses called trulli, *friendly people, wonderful Greek and Roman ruins, and delicious food, especially olive oil, pasta, fish and vegetables. During a food symposium in Lecce, Italy, organized by Oldways Preservation and Exchange Trust, we sampled Apulian pasta dishes of every sort. This humble one is a typical, old-fashioned, home-style kind of dish. You can prepare it with or without the anchovies; it is delicious either way.*

Makes 6 servings

6 ounces fairly stale coarse country bread

1/2 cup olive oil (preferably extra virgin)

3 anchovy fillets (optional)

3 cloves garlic, finely chopped

20 ounces thin spaghetti

Salt and freshly ground white pepper

Trim crust from bread; discard crust. Coarsely crumble bread. You should have about 2 cups.

Heat olive oil in a medium skillet over medium heat. Add anchovies and mash with a fork. Add garlic; cook, stirring frequently, about 3 minutes, or until garlic starts to change color. Add bread crumbs; stir about 2 minutes, or until toasted.

Meanwhile, cook spaghetti *al dente* according to package directions. Drain well.

Put spaghetti on a warmed serving platter. Pour bread crumb sauce over spaghetti. Season to taste with salt and white pepper. Mix gently. Serve immediately.

Vote for tougher drunk driving laws.

Ravioli with Tomato-Olive Sauce

Kathleen Desmond Stang
Free-Lance Food Writer, Seattle, WA

A neat trick for pitting olives is to rap each one with the flat side of a French knife. Place the knife over an olive and pound with your palm to split the olive and loosen the pit. Kalamata olives are more flavorful than plain ripe (black) olives, but canned sliced ripe olives will do in a pinch. Olives are salty, so taste the finished dish to determine if additional salt is necessary.

Makes 2 or 3 servings

2 teaspoons olive oil
1 medium onion, halved and sliced
1 clove garlic, finely chopped
1/4 pound fresh mushrooms
   (4 large)
1 (14 1/2- to 16-ounce) can cut or
   diced tomatoes in purée,
   undrained
About 10 kalamata olives, pitted
   and halved (1/4 cup)

1 tablespoon chopped fresh
   parsley (preferably flat leaf)
1 teaspoon dried basil
1/4 teaspoon black pepper
Salt, to taste
8 ounces refrigerated cheese or
   spinach ravioli
Grated Parmesan cheese

Heat oil in a large skillet over medium-high heat. Add onion and garlic; cook, stirring, 3 or 4 minutes. Add mushrooms; cook, stirring 3 or 4 minutes, or until mushrooms are brown. Add tomatoes with their liquid, olives, parsley, basil, pepper and salt. Reduce heat; let sauce simmer while you cook ravioli.

Cook ravioli according to package directions. Drain well. Add ravioli to tomato-olive sauce; mix gently. Serve in warmed bowls, topped with Parmesan cheese.

Spicy Peanut Butter Noodles

Christine W. Randall
Assistant Features Editor, *The Post and Courier*, Charleston, SC

When I first came across this recipe, it sounded a bit offbeat, but I figured I'd try it once because it was so easy – and I loved it. The original recipe called for creamy peanut butter, but I like the little bit of texture that crunchy peanut butter adds.

Makes 2 to 3 servings

1/3 cup crunchy or smooth peanut butter
2 tablespoons vegetable oil
2 tablespoons soy sauce
1/2 teaspoon cayenne pepper, or to taste

1/2 teaspoon granulated sugar
1 tablespoon balsamic vinegar
1 large clove garlic, finely chopped
8 to 12 ounces spaghetti or linguine

In a bowl, combine peanut butter, oil, soy sauce, cayenne, sugar, vinegar and garlic. With a rubber spatula, work mixture together until creamy and smooth. If time permits, refrigerate, covered, 4 hours. (If you don't have time, don't worry; it will still be good.) Bring to room temperature before using.

Cook spaghetti according to package directions. Drain well. Combine hot cooked pasta and peanut butter sauce; mix gently. Serve immediately.

Spinach and Ziti Bake

Delia A. Hammock
Nutrition and Fitness Editor, *Good Housekeeping*, New York, NY

This recipe was created on a snowy evening when I had a serious craving for hearty Italian food but didn't want to venture outside. It has remained a favorite because it's easy to toss together and it's not loaded with fat. Add a crusty loaf of bread and you have a great meal.

Makes 4 servings

8 ounces ziti (2 cups)
1 (10-ounce) package frozen
  chopped spinach, thawed
  and squeezed dry
1/2 (15-ounce) carton part-skim
  ricotta cheese
1 (14-ounce) jar spaghetti sauce
  with mushrooms

1 egg, lightly beaten
1/3 cup grated Parmesan cheese
1 teaspoon salt
1/2 teaspoon dried oregano
1/4 teaspoon freshly ground
  black pepper

Cook ziti according to package directions. Drain well.

In a large bowl, combine ziti, spinach, ricotta cheese, spaghetti sauce, egg, Parmesan cheese, salt, oregano and pepper; mix well.

Spray a 1 1/2-quart baking dish with vegetable cooking spray. Spoon ziti mixture into baking dish. Bake in a preheated 350° oven 25 to 30 minutes, or until top is golden brown and sauce is bubbly.

Winter Vegetable Stir-Fry

Anita Stewart
Executive Director, *Cuisine Canada*, Elora, Ontario, Canada

This is THE meal that my university guys make for themselves — long on flavor and short on time. It's one of those basic recipes that, with a little imagination, can be stretched to feed the multitudes by adding extra cooked pasta. For non-vegetarians, add chopped cooked sausage, ham or chicken, if desired.

Makes 6 to 8 servings

12 ounces penne or elbow macaroni (3 cups)
4 tablespoons olive oil, divided
4 cloves garlic, finely chopped
1 large onion, sliced
2 to 3 carrots, sliced diagonally
1 bunch broccoli (about 1 pound), trimmed and cut into florets
1/4 cup water
1/2 green or red bell pepper, thinly sliced

1/2 pound fresh mushrooms, sliced
1/4 cup soy sauce
1/2 to 1 teaspoon crushed red pepper (or 1 jalapeño pepper, seeded and finely chopped)
1 1/2 teaspoons freshly ground black pepper
2 cups grated Monterey Jack cheese (8 ounces)

Cook pasta according to package directions. Drain well. Mix pasta with 1 tablespoon of the oil; set aside.

Heat remaining 3 tablespoons oil in a large skillet. Add garlic and onion; cook, stirring, over medium-high heat 1 minute. Add carrots; cook, stirring, 1 minute. Add broccoli and water; steam, covered, 2 to 3 minutes, or until broccoli is bright green. Uncover; add bell pepper and mushrooms. Cook, stirring, until tender-crisp. Season with soy sauce, red pepper flakes and black pepper. Add reserved pasta; stir until pasta is thoroughly reheated.

Sprinkle a generous portion of cheese on each serving. Pass extra soy sauce or hot peanut sauce at the table, if desired.

Find out how your state "rates" on drunk driving legislation.

Cheese, Eggs *and* Beans

Black Beans International

Christine W. Randall
Assistant Features Editor, *The Post and Courier*, Charleston, SC

I'm not the kind of cook who plans menus a week ahead of time. How can I possibly know on Sunday what I'll want to eat on Friday? Therefore, I'm a great fan of recipes that are easy to prepare and use ingredients that I have on hand. This one fills the bill perfectly, and easily can be halved if you don't need six servings.

Makes 6 servings

8 ounces orzo (2 cups)
3 tablespoons olive oil
1/2 cup chopped onion
2 cloves garlic, crushed

2 (16-ounce) cans black beans, drained
1/2 teaspoon dried oregano
3 tablespoons balsamic vinegar

Cook orzo according to package directions. Drain well. Meanwhile, heat olive oil in a large skillet. Add onion and garlic; cook, stirring, until onion is soft. Stir in black beans, oregano and balsamic vinegar. Simmer, covered, until heated through. Serve over hot orzo.

Please say "crash," not "accident," when talking about alcohol-related collisions.

Blue Cheese Noodles

Carolyn Flournoy
Food Columnist, *The Times*, Shreveport, LA

My favorite noodle recipe was born because of an overabundance of Roquefort cheese, which we had received as a gift. After quarts of Roquefort salad dressing, my family cried, "Enough!" While cooking noodles one day, I created the following recipe, which was an instant success. However, after we ran out of the Roquefort, I turned to American blue cheese for economy's sake and it's just as good.

Makes 8 to 10 servings

1/2 cup butter or margarine	16 ounces fine egg noodles
8 to 10 green onions, chopped	(10 cups)
4 ounces blue cheese	1/2 teaspoon vegetable oil
1 1/2 (8-ounce) cartons sour cream	1 tablespoon chicken bouillon
Seasoned pepper, to taste	granules

Melt butter in a large heavy skillet. Add green onions; cook, stirring, until onions are golden. Crumble blue cheese into onion mixture. Stir over medium heat until cheese is melted. Remove from heat. Stir in sour cream and seasoned pepper.

Meanwhile, cook noodles according to package directions, adding oil and chicken bouillon granules to boiling water. Drain well.

Stir noodles into sauce. For best results, cover and let stand several hours for flavors to blend. Reheat slowly (or heat in a microwave oven) before serving.

Note: If desired, add finely chopped garlic and/or sliced ripe olives to taste.

Chocolate Dessert Pasta

Paula M. Galusha
Free-Lance Home Economist, Tulsa, OK

Most dessert pasta recipes add high-calorie sauces to the pasta. This is unfortunate because the pasta itself is low in fat, high in carbohydrates and has no sugar or salt. This dessert features a low-fat chocolate sauce. Serve it with regular or chocolate fettuccine, which is available at gourmet or health food stores.

Makes 4 servings

8 ounces regular or chocolate
fettuccine
2 cups skim milk, divided
2 tablespoons cornstarch

1/4 cup unsweetened cocoa powder
1/4 cup granulated sugar
1/2 teaspoon ground cinnamon
Vanilla yogurt

Cook fettuccine according to package directions. Drain well. Put in a large bowl.

Meanwhile, combine 1/4 cup of the milk and cornstarch in a small saucepan; mix until smooth. Stir in cocoa powder, sugar, cinnamon and remaining 13/4 cups milk; mix well. Heat just to boiling, stirring constantly; cook 1 minute, or until sauce is thickened.

Pour chocolate sauce over pasta; mix gently. Top individual servings with a dollop of yogurt.

Please don't laugh at or tell stories that treat drunk driving humorously.

Dessert Kugel

Beth W. Orenstein
Free-Lance Writer, Northampton, PA

Although kugel is traditionally served as a side dish, this recipe tastes just like cheesecake, so it easily can be served as a dessert. I had an editor who loved it so much that I could get good assignments from her if I brought her some leftovers whenever my mother made it. It's as delicious cold as it is warm. For dessert, serve it straight from the refrigerator, topped with fresh fruit in season.

Makes 6 to 8 servings

8 ounces fine egg noodles (5 cups)
1 cup margarine
8 eggs, lightly beaten
1 (8-ounce) package cream
cheese, softened

2 cups sour cream
1 cup granulated sugar
2 teaspoons vanilla extract

Cook noodles according to package directions. Drain well.

Meanwhile, melt margarine in a 13x9x2-inch baking pan. Swirl to coat pan. Arrange noodles on melted margarine in pan.

In large bowl of electric mixer, combine eggs, cream cheese, sour cream, sugar and vanilla; mix well. Pour egg mixture over noodles.

Bake, uncovered, in a preheated 350° oven 1 hour, or until set. Serve warm; or refrigerate, covered, and serve chilled.

Garlic Noodles

Lorrie Guttman
Food Editor, *Tallahassee Democrat*, Tallahassee, FL

This recipe received honorable mention in a "Capital Chef" contest sponsored by my newspaper. It's actually a baked, garlicky variation of Fettuccine Alfredo. Once the initial preparation is done, you simply slip the casserole into the oven and let it bake. The original recipe called for ½ cup butter; you can use half that much, as I've indicated. You can use low-fat or nonfat sour cream to make the recipe even less sinful.

Makes 8 to 10 servings

16 ounces egg or spinach noodles (10 cups)
¼ cup butter or margarine
¼ cup olive oil
4 large cloves garlic, pressed
½ cup grated Parmesan cheese
Salt and freshly ground black pepper, to taste
2 cups sour cream
Chopped fresh parsley

Cook noodles according to package directions. Drain well.

Meanwhile, melt butter in large saucepan. Add olive oil and garlic; cook, stirring, until garlic is light brown. Add noodles, Parmesan cheese, salt and pepper; mix well. Stir in sour cream.

Spray a 13x9x2-inch baking pan with vegetable cooking spray. Spoon mixture into pan. Sprinkle chopped parsley on top. Cover with aluminum foil. Bake in a preheated 325° oven about 30 minutes, or until hot and bubbly. Serve immediately.

Lasagna al Forno

Janet Geissler
Food Editor, *Lansing State Journal*, Lansing, MI

If you are looking for good sources of protein while cutting back on meat, consider nuts. Here's an unusual lasagna that uses walnuts instead of meat. I like to prepare this recipe with whole wheat-soy lasagna noodles (available in health food stores and some supermarkets) for an extra nutrition boost.

Makes 4 to 6 servings

12 ounces whole wheat-soy or plain lasagna noodles
1 medium bunch fresh spinach
3 cups tomato sauce
1/2 cup chopped walnuts, almonds or sunflower seeds, toasted
1 cup cottage cheese (or 3/4 cup ricotta cheese mixed with 1/2 cup skim milk)
1/4 cup grated Parmesan cheese
12 thin slices mozzarella or Swiss cheese

Cook noodles according to package directions. Drain well.

Rinse spinach in cold water and remove stems. Drain well. Chop or tear into bite-size pieces.

Spread 3/4 cup tomato sauce in an 8x8x2-inch baking pan. Place one-third of the noodles over sauce. Cover noodles with one-third of the spinach, 2 tablespoons walnuts, 1/4 cup cottage cheese, 1 tablespoon Parmesan cheese and 3 slices mozzarella cheese. Repeat layers twice. Spread the remaining 3/4 cup tomato sauce, remaining 2 tablespoons walnuts, remaining 1/4 cup cottage cheese, remaining 1 tablespoon Parmesan cheese, and remaining 3 slices mozzarella cheese on top.

Bake in a preheated 350° oven 40 minutes, or until hot and bubbly. Let stand 10 minutes before serving.

Note: To toast walnuts, almonds or sunflower seeds, spread them on an ungreased baking sheet. Bake in a preheated 350° oven 5 to 7 minutes, stirring occasionally, or until light brown.

Light-Style Fettuccine Alfredo

Beth W. Orenstein
Free-Lance Writer, Northampton, PA

We've been cooking light since some members of our family were diagnosed with high cholesterol. Pasta is a favorite food, but we've reduced the fat in many of the sauces. This recipe calls for nonfat cream cheese and Parmesan cheese, but you can use low-fat or regular, if you prefer. This dish is tasty either way.

Makes 3 to 4 servings

12 ounces fettuccine
1 tablespoon margarine
2 cloves garlic, finely chopped
1 tablespoon all-purpose flour
1½ cups skim milk

2 tablespoons nonfat cream cheese
1 cup grated nonfat or part-skim milk Parmesan cheese
2 teaspoons chopped fresh parsley

Cook fettuccine according to package directions. Drain well.

Meanwhile, melt margarine in a large skillet. Add garlic; cook, stirring, 1 minute. Stir in flour. Gradually add milk, stirring with a whisk, until blended. Cook, stirring, 5 minutes, or until thickened and bubbly. Stir in cream cheese; cook 2 minutes. Add Parmesan cheese; stir until cheese is melted.

Put pasta in a large warmed serving bowl. Pour sauce over pasta; mix gently. Sprinkle with parsley. Serve immediately.

Remind teens that underage drinking is dangerous and against the law.

Lukshen Kugel

Lorrie Guttman
Food Editor, *Tallahassee Democrat*, Tallahassee, FL

I have fond memories of the lukshen kugel (noodle pudding) that my mother sometimes served for dessert when I was a child. The firm noodles accented by puffy baked raisins and cinnamon sugar made a nourishing, comforting end to the meal. Mom says Grandma made her lukshen kugel this way – very simply, instead of with the cottage cheese and/or cream cheese often used in noodle puddings. Recently I've discovered that this kugel also is delicious as a change of pace for breakfast.

Makes 9 servings

12 ounces wide egg noodles
(7 1/2 cups)
3 eggs, lightly beaten
1/4 teaspoon salt

1 cup raisins
1/4 cup granulated sugar
2 teaspoons ground cinnamon

Cook noodles according to package directions. Drain, then rinse with cold water. Drain well.

In a large bowl, combine eggs and salt; beat well. Add noodles; stir until well mixed. Stir in raisins.

Spray an 8x8x2-inch baking pan with vegetable cooking spray. Spoon noodle mixture into pan. Combine sugar and cinnamon in a small bowl; sprinkle over noodles.

Bake, uncovered, in a preheated 325° oven 25 minutes. Remove from oven and let stand 5 minutes before serving.

Pasta with Cannellini

Narcisse S. Cadgène
Free-Lance Writer, New York, NY

Pasta Fazool, or pasta with white kidney beans, was never so elegant, or, thanks to canned beans, so easy. Fresh sage lends a wonderful, full-bodied flavor to the beans. If fresh sage is not available, substitute up to half the amount of whole dried sage leaves; do not use ground sage for this dish.

Makes 6 servings

8 ounces bow tie pasta (4 cups)
2 tablespoons olive oil
2 ounces prosciutto or cooked
  ham, finely chopped
1 medium onion, sliced
4 cloves garlic, crushed
2 tablespoons chopped fresh
  sage leaves

1 (16-ounce) can cannellini
  (white beans), drained
Salt and black pepper
Grated Parmesan or Romano
  cheese

Cook pasta according to package directions. Drain well.

Heat oil in a large skillet. Add prosciutto, onion and garlic; cook, stirring, over low heat about 8 minutes, or until onion is soft but not brown.

Add sage, beans and pasta; cook, stirring gently, until everything is heated through. Season to taste with salt and pepper. Serve immediately, topped with Parmesan cheese. Or, serve at room temperature, usually without cheese.

Drunk driving deaths among 15- to 19-year-olds decreased nearly 60% since 1982.

Pasta with Creamy Cheese Sauce

Alice Handkins
Free-Lance Food Writer, Wichita, KS

One of my favorite pasta sauces is this rich, creamy blend of golden Gouda, buttery-tasting Gruyère, nutty-tasting Fontina and mellow Provolone cheeses. I like to serve this sauce over angel hair pasta, but it also is delicious over spinach fettuccine or any pasta of choice. Although the sauce is deliciously elegant, it is quick and simple to prepare.

Makes 3 cups sauce; enough for 6 servings of pasta

2 tablespoons butter
1 tablespoon all-purpose flour
1 1/2 cups heavy cream
3 ounces Gouda cheese, coarsely grated (3/4 cup)
3 ounces Gruyère cheese, coarsely grated (3/4 cup)
3 ounces Fontina cheese, coarsely grated (3/4 cup)
3 ounces Provolone cheese, coarsely grated (3/4 cup)
Hot cooked pasta
Fresh parsley sprigs
Freshly grated Parmesan cheese
Freshly ground black pepper

Melt butter in a saucepan over medium heat. Stir in flour. Slowly add cream, stirring constantly. Continue heating and stirring until the sauce thickens. Add Gouda, Gruyère, Fontina and Provolone cheeses. Cook, stirring, over medium heat until cheeses melt and sauce is hot. Do not let sauce boil.

Serve sauce over your favorite pasta. Garnish each serving with a sprig of parsley, a generous sprinkling of Parmesan cheese and lots of pepper, if desired. Serve immediately.

Peach Noodle Kugel

Lorrie Guttman
Food Editor, *Tallahassee Democrat*, Tallahassee, FL

My mother can't remember where she got this recipe; it's one that's tattered from years of use. Although this noodle pudding is somewhat sweet, it makes a good side dish for a simple fish or poultry entrée. You also could serve it for dessert. The streusel topping is a bit unusual, with its combination of bread crumbs and cinnamon.

Makes 8 to 10 servings

16 ounces wide egg noodles
    (10 cups)
3 tablespoons margarine, melted
3 eggs, lightly beaten
1/2 cup granulated sugar
1 1/2 tablespoons grated lemon peel
1/4 teaspoon salt
2 cups milk
1/2 cup raisins
1 (16-ounce) can sliced peaches,
    drained

Streusel Topping:
2 tablespoons margarine
1/4 cup dry bread crumbs
1 tablespoon ground cinnamon

Cook noodles according to package directions. Drain well. Return noodles to cooking pot or put in a large bowl. Add margarine; stir to coat noodles.

In a medium bowl, combine eggs, sugar, lemon peel and salt; mix well. Stir in milk and raisins. Pour egg mixture over noodles; stir gently until well combined.

Spray a 13x9x2-inch baking pan with vegetable cooking spray. Spoon noodle mixture into pan. Bake, uncovered, in a preheated 325° oven 30 minutes.

While kugel is baking, prepare the streusel topping. Melt margarine in a small saucepan. Add bread crumbs and cinnamon; mix well.

Remove kugel from oven. Arrange peach slices on top; sprinkle streusel topping on peaches. Return to oven. Bake 15 minutes, or until hot and bubbly. Let stand at least 15 minutes before serving.

Sassy Spaghetti

Lorrie Guttman
Food Editor, *Tallahassee Democrat*, Tallahassee, FL

I whipped up this main dish one day when I had about 15 minutes to put dinner on the table. Later, I submitted it to the food editors' competition in the Newman's Own Third Annual Recipe Contest, co-sponsored by Good Housekeeping magazine. I won honorable mention, worth $2,500 for my chosen charity, Hadassah. Needless to say, the recipe is still a favorite of mine, just the thing when I need a quick, easy, nutritious entree from ingredients I keep on hand.

Makes 4 servings

8 ounces spaghetti
1 (11-ounce) jar medium-hot salsa
1 (4-ounce) can mushroom stems and pieces, drained
1 (15-ounce) can black beans, rinsed and drained

Finely grated Monterey Jack cheese
1 lime, cut into 4 wedges (or about 2 tablespoons lime juice)

Cook spaghetti al dente according to package directions. Drain well.

Meanwhile, in a large saucepan, combine salsa, mushrooms and black beans; mix well. Simmer, covered, to let flavors blend.

Ladle sauce over individual servings of spaghetti; top with grated cheese and garnish with lime wedge. Just before eating, squeeze lime juice over spaghetti.

Sweet Noodles

Debra Carr-Elsing
Food Writer, *The Capital Times*, Madison, WI

When I tell people how few ingredients are in this elegant dessert, they're always surprised by the dish's utter simplicity. Recipes don't have to be complicated to be delicious.

Makes 4 servings

8 ounces wide egg noodles
   (5 cups) or fettucine
1/2 cup honey
1/4 cup butter

1 teaspoon ground cinnamon
1/4 cup chopped walnuts or
   2 tablespoons poppy seeds

Cook noodles according to package directions. Drain well. Divide noodles among 4 serving plates.

While pasta is cooking, combine honey, butter and cinnamon in a small saucepan. Cook, stirring, until butter is melted.

Drizzle warm butter mixture over hot noodles; sprinkle nuts on top. Serve immediately.

Note: If you don't want to do all the cooking for this dessert in the middle of dinner, cook the noodles in advance, rinse with cold water, and drain well. When ready to serve, put noodles in a strainer and dip in boiling water just long enough to reheat, about 30 seconds. Drain well.

Tell your legislators that you endorse a .00 blood alcohol content for youths under 21.

Macaroni *and* Cheese

Easiest Macaroni and Cheese

Arlette Camp Copeland
Food Writer, *The Macon Telegraph*, Macon, GA

My oldest daughter learned to love macaroni and cheese at my mother's house. I never prepared it because it was not a dish I liked as a child. As I grew older and my tastes changed, one day it struck me that I'd like to have some of mother's macaroni and cheese. I didn't have the slightest idea how to make it. I looked at recipes that included egg and milk and other ingredients. I wasn't impressed. The simple recipe I created can be used as a side dish or, if you add meat, it's a good main dish. It's also good with sauteed mushrooms.

Makes 4 to 6 servings

8 ounces elbow macaroni (2 cups)
  or spiral pasta (3 cups)
3 cups shredded cheese
  (a mixture of cheeses is best)

1/4 cup butter
Salt and black pepper

Prepare pasta according to package directions. Drain well. Return to hot cooking pot. Add cheese and butter to hot pasta; stir until cheese and butter are melted. (The heat of the pasta and the pot should be enough to melt cheese and butter. If necessary, cook over low heat 1 to 2 minutes, stirring constantly.) Season to taste with salt and pepper. Serve immediately.

Educate youngsters about the dangers of alcohol and other drug use.

Favorite Macaroni and Cheese

Teri M. Grimes
Features Editor, *The Bradenton Herald*, Bradenton, FL

No compilation of pasta recipes would be complete without one for macaroni and cheese. It's probably the first pasta dish we're introduced to as children, and the one we take the most comfort in as adults. This version is fancy enough for company. In fact, if you throw in leftover cooked chicken or ham, bite-size vegetables or even bread cubes, you'll have a worthy main dish.

Makes 6 servings

8 ounces elbow macaroni (2 cups)
1/4 cup plus 1 tablespoon butter, divided
1 small onion, finely chopped
1/4 cup all-purpose flour
1 cup milk
1 1/2 cups grated mild Cheddar cheese (6 ounces)
1 teaspoon Worcestershire sauce
1/2 teaspoon salt
1 cup sour cream, at room temperature
1/2 pound bacon, cooked crisp and crumbled
1/4 cup dry bread crumbs

Cook macaroni according to package directions. Drain well.

Melt 1/4 cup of the butter in a large saucepan. Add onion; cook, stirring, until onion is softened. Stir in flour; cook, stirring, 1 minute. Slowly add milk, stirring constantly; cook until sauce thickens. Add cheese, Worcestershire sauce and salt; cook, stirring, until cheese melts. Remove from heat. Gradually add sour cream to sauce, stirring constantly. Gently stir in macaroni.

Spoon mixture into a greased 2-quart baking pan. Sprinkle bacon on top. Melt the remaining 1 tablespoon butter; add bread crumbs and stir to mix. Sprinkle crumb mixture over bacon. Bake, uncovered, in a preheated 375° oven 25 to 30 minutes, or until bubbly.

Macaroni and Cheese Bake

Sally L. Scherer
Staff Writer, *The Macon Telegraph*, Macon, GA

My sister makes the best homemade macaroni and cheese in the world, but the recipe she uses is lengthy and complex. For years, I assumed macaroni and cheese was too difficult to prepare from scratch. Then I found this recipe. I usually have all the ingredients on hand.

Makes 4 to 6 servings

8 ounces elbow macaroni (2 cups)
2 tablespoons margarine
1/3 cup thinly sliced green onions
3 tablespoons all-purpose flour
2 1/4 cups skim milk, divided
1 cup shredded sharp Cheddar cheese (4 ounces)
1/4 teaspoon dry mustard
1/8 teaspoon black pepper
1/8 teaspoon hot pepper sauce
1/4 cup fresh whole wheat bread crumbs
2 tablespoons grated Parmesan cheese
1/8 teaspoon paprika

Cook macaroni according to package directions. Drain well.

Meanwhile, melt margarine in a large saucepan over medium heat. Add green onions; cook, stirring, 2 minutes, or until tender. Add flour; cook, stirring constantly with a whisk, 1 minute. Gradually add 2 cups of the milk; cook, stirring, 5 to 10 minutes, or until mixture thickens. Remove from heat. Add Cheddar cheese; stir until cheese melts. Stir in remaining 1/4 cup milk, dry mustard, pepper and hot pepper sauce. Add macaroni; mix gently.

Spray a 1 1/2-quart baking pan with vegetable cooking spray. Spoon macaroni mixture into pan. Combine bread crumbs, Parmesan cheese and paprika; sprinkle over macaroni. Bake, uncovered, in a preheated 350° oven 30 minutes, or until hot and bubbly.

Help young people learn why they shouldn't drink while they are under 21.

Macaroni and Cheese with Tomato

Lori Longbotham
Free-Lance Food Writer, New York, NY

I don't know anyone who doesn't like macaroni and cheese, especially children. We carry that fondness into adulthood; it comforted us then and it comforts us now. This is a simple, old-fashioned version. The tomato makes it taste and look better than traditional macaroni and cheese.

Makes 6 servings

12 ounces elbow macaroni (3 cups)
3 tablespoons butter
3 tablespoons all-purpose flour
1 3/4 cups milk
1 cup chicken broth
1/2 cup drained chopped canned plum (Roma) tomatoes
1 teaspoon salt
1/2 teaspoon freshly ground black pepper
1 1/2 cups shredded Cheddar cheese (6 ounces), divided
1 cup shredded Swiss cheese (4 ounces)
1/2 cup grated Parmesan cheese

Cook macaroni al dente according to package directions. Drain well.

Meanwhile, melt butter in a medium saucepan over medium-low heat. Add flour; stir until smooth. Reduce heat to low. Cook, stirring constantly, 3 minutes. Gradually whisk in milk and broth. Heat, stirring constantly, until mixture simmers. Stir in tomatoes, salt and pepper. Simmer, uncovered, stirring occasionally, 5 minutes. Remove from heat. Add 1 cup of the Cheddar cheese, the Swiss cheese and Parmesan cheese; mix well.

In a large bowl, combine macaroni and cheese sauce; mix gently. Spoon mixture into a greased 2 1/2-quart shallow baking pan. Bake, uncovered, in a preheated 400° oven 15 minutes. Remove from oven; carefully stir mixture. Sprinkle the remaining 1/2 cup Cheddar cheese on top. Return to oven and bake 15 minutes, or until bubbly and golden brown. Let stand 2 to 3 minutes before serving.

Microwave Macaroni and Cheese

Monetta L. Harr
Food Writer, *Jackson Citizen Patriot*, Jackson, MI

This recipe was printed in the Jackson Citizen Patriot *years ago, long before I became the food writer. But with two toddlers at home, I knew an easy recipe when I saw it. The recipe is tucked away in my recipe file and now my son and daughter are old enough to prepare the recipe themselves. It is usually a Saturday lunch, and is definitely preferred over boxed macaroni and cheese mixes. Not only does it taste better than boxed, but it also is more convenient because it cooks in the microwave.*

Makes 4 servings

6 ounces elbow macaroni
(1 1/2 cups)
1 1/2 tablespoons all-purpose flour
1 teaspoon salt
1 1/2 cups water

1 cup milk
2 tablespoons margarine
1 cup shredded Cheddar cheese
(4 ounces)

In a greased 2-quart microwave-safe baking dish, combine uncooked macaroni, flour and salt; stir to coat macaroni with flour. Add water, milk and margarine; mix well. Cover and microwave on High (100% power) 6 to 7 minutes, or until mixture boils. Let stand 5 minutes. Stir in cheese. Microwave on High 3 to 4 minutes, or until mixture boils and thickens. Let stand a few minutes before serving.

Tell the young people in your life about MADD's Poster/Essay Contest.

Mexican Macaroni and Cheese

Carolyn Flournoy
Food Columnist, *The Times*, Shreveport, LA

Although we live in Louisiana, we're only 12 miles from the Texas state line. Hence, my four kids grew up eating a lot more Tex-Mex food than Creole and Cajun dishes. One of my inspirations for a piñata birthday party was Mexican Macaroni and Cheese, which was a hit with both the younger set and their parents. A local Mexican restaurant adapted my recipe and now serves it, too. Ole!

Makes 4 to 6 servings

8 ounces elbow macaroni (2 cups)
1/4 cup margarine
3 tablespoons all-purpose flour
1 teaspoon finely chopped garlic
    or 1/4 teaspoon garlic powder
1/2 teaspoon salt
1/4 teaspoon black pepper
3 cups milk
1/4 cup finely chopped onion

1 (4-ounce) can chopped green
    chilies, drained
1 (2-ounce) jar chopped
    pimentos, drained
3 cups shredded Monterey Jack
    cheese (12 ounces)
1/2 cup crushed corn chips or
    tortillas
Paprika, to taste

Cook macaroni *al dente* according to package directions. Drain well.

Melt margarine in a large saucepan. Blend in flour, garlic, salt and pepper. Cook, stirring constantly, 1 to 2 minutes. Slowly add milk, stirring until smooth. Add onion, chilies and pimentos; cook, stirring constantly, until thickened. Stir in cheese; cook, stirring, until cheese is melted. Add macaroni; mix gently.

Spoon mixture into a greased 3-quart baking dish. Sprinkle crushed corn chips and paprika on top. Bake, uncovered, in a preheated 350° oven 25 minutes, or until hot and bubbly. Serve immediately.

Mother's Macaroni and Cheese

Kasey Wilson
Food Columnist, *The Vancouver Courier*, Vancouver, BC, Canada

My twin sister, Karen, and I loved it when our dad went out of town because our mom would prepare casseroles for dinner instead of meat and potatoes. Dad didn't know what he was missing. This was our favorite dish and there were never any leftovers.

Makes 4 to 6 servings

5 ounces shell macaroni (2 cups)
3 tablespoons butter
3 tablespoons all-purpose flour
1 cup heavy cream
1 cup milk
3 tablespoons cream cheese,
   at room temperature

2 cups grated medium Cheddar
   cheese (8 ounces), divided
3 green onions, finely chopped
1/2 green bell pepper, chopped
2 tomatoes, chopped
1 teaspoon salt

Cook macaroni according to package directions. Drain, then rinse with cool water. Drain well.

Meanwhile, melt butter in a large saucepan over medium-low heat. Add flour; stir with a whisk 3 to 4 minutes. Gradually add cream and milk; stir until sauce thickens. Add cream cheese and 1 1/2 cups of the Cheddar cheese; stir just until blended. Remove from heat. Add green onions, bell pepper, tomatoes, salt and macaroni; mix gently.

Spoon mixture into a greased 13x9x2-inch baking pan. Sprinkle remaining 1/2 cup Cheddar cheese on top. Bake, uncovered, in a preheated 350° oven 30 minutes, or until hot and bubbly. Serve immediately.

Talk to the young people in your life if you think they are using alcohol.

Southern Macaroni and Cheese

Jeanne Voltz
Cookbook Author, Pittsboro, NC

Macaroni baked in a custard fragrant with real cheese was the standard in Southern farm kitchens. The cheese was available at country stores and fresh eggs and milk were from the farm. I make a reasonable facsimile using well-aged commercial Cheddar cheese that is labeled "extra sharp." The flavors of natural dairy foods with the bland macaroni made this a favorite main dish with garden vegetables.

Makes 4 servings

8 ounces elbow macaroni (2 cups)
1 tablespoon butter
3 cups coarsely shredded
    sharp Cheddar cheese
    (12 ounces), divided

1 cup milk
2 eggs, lightly beaten
1/2 teaspoon salt, or to taste
1/8 teaspoon black pepper

Cook macaroni *al dente* according to package directions. Drain well. Return macaroni to cooking pot. Add butter; mix gently until butter melts. Add 2 1/2 cups of the cheese; mix lightly. Spoon mixture into a greased 1 1/2-quart baking dish.

In a small bowl, combine milk, eggs, salt and pepper; mix well. Pour over the macaroni mixture. Sprinkle the remaining 1/2 cup cheese on top. Bake, uncovered, in a preheated 325° oven 30 minutes, or until custard is set and cheese on top has melted. Serve immediately.

The Ultimate Macaroni and Cheese

Anita Stewart
Executive Director, *Cuisine Canada*, Elora, Ontario, Canada

This is the creamiest macaroni and cheese ever created, an honest-to-goodness comfort food. My mother always served it with homemade chili sauce.

Makes 4 to 6 servings

8 ounces elbow macaroni (2 cups)
1/2 cup butter, divided
3 tablespoons all-purpose flour
1 teaspoon dry mustard
3/4 teaspoon salt
1/2 teaspoon freshly ground
    black pepper
2 cups milk, heated
1 medium onion, finely chopped
2 cups shredded medium or sharp
    Cheddar cheese (8 ounces)
1 cup soft bread crumbs

Cook macaroni according to package directions. Drain well.

Melt 1/4 cup of the butter in a large saucepan. Stir in flour, dry mustard, salt and pepper. Cook, stirring, until bubbly. Slowly whisk in milk and onion; cook, stirring, 5 minutes, or until thickened. Add cheese; stir until melted. Add macaroni; mix gently. Spoon mixture into a greased 1 1/2-quart baking dish.

Melt the remaining 1/4 cup butter in a skillet. Add bread crumbs; cook, stirring, until golden. Sprinkle crumbs over macaroni.

Bake, uncovered, in a preheated 400° oven 20 minutes, or until hot and bubbly. Serve immediately.

Arrests for DWI were highest among the 30-34 year-old age group in 1993.

Soups *and* Salads

Artichoke Pasta Salad

Barbara Yost
Feature Writer, *The Phoenix Gazette*, Phoenix, AZ

*My recipe card for this wonderful salad is so stained and battered I can
barely read it. Fortunately, I've made it so many times I almost have it
memorized. This is delicious, and is also a sentimental favorite of mine.
The original recipe came from my friend Ann Johnson. When she moved
to California years ago, this was all she left behind -- and the memories
of the times we ate it together. It's best served cold with crusty bread or
rolls, but it also can be heated in a microwave oven and served hot. Just
don't zap it too long, to avoid overheating the mayonnaise.*

Makes 6 servings

8 ounces tri-color spiral pasta
    (3 cups)
1 tablespoon olive oil
1 (8-ounce) jar marinated
    artichoke hearts, undrained
1/2 cup Italian salad dressing
3 cloves garlic, finely chopped
1/2 cup chopped broccoli,
    cooked

1/2 cup frozen green peas, thawed
10 cherry tomatoes, halved
1 (6-ounce) can pitted ripe olives,
    halved
1 cup mayonnaise
2 tablespoons distilled white vinegar
Salt and black pepper

Cook pasta according to package directions, adding the olive oil to
the cooking water. Drain well. Put pasta in a large bowl. Pour the
marinade from the artichokes over the pasta. Add salad dressing and
garlic; mix well. Add artichokes, cooked broccoli, peas (it is not
necessary to cook them), tomatoes and olives.

In a small bowl, combine mayonnaise and vinegar. Stir into pasta
mixture; mix gently. Season to taste with salt and pepper. Refrigerate,
covered, overnight, or until serving time.

Never ride with an alcohol-impaired driver — no matter how old you are.

Broccoli-Ramen Noodle Slaw

Barbara Gibbs Ostmann
Food Writer, St. Louis, MO

Marcelyn Brown of Springdale, Ark., a long-time family friend, served this salad at a summer picnic and everyone asked for the recipe, including me. I have since served it at numerous picnics and barbecues, always to rave reviews. I solved the problem of recipe requests by printing several copies, so they're handy whenever anyone asks for the recipe. One friend, who had eaten this at my sister's home and got the recipe from her, made the recipe with sunflower seeds still in the shell — that's a little too much dietary fiber! Be sure to use the shelled variety.

Makes 6 to 8 servings

2 (3-ounce) packages Oriental-flavored instant ramen noodles (see note)
1 (16-ounce) package broccoli slaw (see note)
1 cup slivered or sliced almonds
1/2 to 1 cup shelled sunflower seeds (salted or unsalted)

Dressing:
1/2 cup granulated sugar
3/4 cup vegetable oil
1/4 cup red wine vinegar
2 packets seasoning mix (from the ramen noodle packages)

Remove seasoning packets from noodles; reserve for use in dressing. Coarsely crumble the dry noodles. Combine noodles and broccoli slaw in a large bowl. Stir in almonds and sunflower seeds.

For dressing, combine sugar, oil, vinegar and noodle seasoning mix in a small saucepan; mix well. Heat over low heat, stirring occasionally, until mixture simmers.

Pour dressing over broccoli mixture; mix well. Refrigerate, covered, until serving time; stir occasionally to thoroughly mix dressing and slaw.

Note: You can substitute any flavor of ramen noodle, but Oriental flavor is specified in the original recipe. Broccoli slaw is a mixture of julienned broccoli, carrots and red cabbage; available in plastic bags in the produce section of most supermarkets. If you're out of red wine vinegar, you can substitute lemon juice.

Chinese Pasta Salad

Lori Longbotham
Free-Lance Food Writer, New York, NY

This has more flavor and better texture than the Chinese take-out some of us resort to when we think we just don't have time to cook dinner--and it's much more healthful. But the important thing is that you can have it ready in less time than the guy on the bicycle can deliver. Make it tonight and consider the possibility of doubling the recipe and taking some to work tomorrow for lunch.

Makes 4 servings

1/2 cup chicken broth
1 whole chicken breast, skinned, boned and cut into thin strips
2 green onions, thinly sliced
1 small red bell pepper, thinly sliced
1 clove garlic, finely chopped

1 teaspoon finely chopped fresh ginger
1/4 cup low-sodium soy sauce
2 teaspoons sesame oil
1/4 teaspoon crushed red pepper
8 ounces spaghettini or spaghetti

Bring broth to boiling in a medium skillet over medium-high heat. Add chicken; cook about 3 minutes, or until firm to the touch. Remove chicken; strain broth and reserve. In a large bowl, combine chicken, green onions, bell pepper and garlic.

In a small bowl, whisk together ginger, soy sauce, sesame oil, red pepper flakes and reserved broth.

Meanwhile, cook pasta according to package directions. Drain well. Add pasta to chicken mixture. Pour ginger mixture over all; mix gently. Serve warm.

Please remember to say, "No, thanks" to alcohol if you're driving.

Gingered Cauliflower, Broccoli and Pasta Soup

Julie Watson
Cookbook Author, Charlottetown, Prince Edward Island, Canada

This family soup is traditionally made with barley to give it body. It has been updated to fit the tastes and lifestyle of today by the addition of pasta and the tangy fresh herb, cilantro. Pasta complements the rich broth and creates a thicker, more satisfying soup. Both the cilantro and ginger are dominant tastes, so you might want to reduce the amounts to suit your own preference.

Makes 4 to 6 servings

1/2 cup pearl barley
1 tablespoon olive oil
1 medium onion, finely chopped
2 cloves garlic, crushed
1 tablespoon finely chopped
    fresh ginger
1/2 teaspoon ground turmeric
1 teaspoon coriander seeds,
    crushed

1 teaspoon cumin seeds
1 large carrot, thickly sliced
7 1/2 cups vegetable broth
4 ounces elbow macaroni or
    3 ounces shell macaroni or
    tri-color spiral pasta (1 cup)
3 cups cauliflower and/or
    broccoli florets
1/4 cup chopped fresh cilantro

Cover barley with boiling water and let stand 1 hour. Drain well.

Meanwhile, heat oil in a large skillet. Add onion and garlic; cook, stirring, until soft. Add ginger, turmeric, coriander seeds and cumin seeds. Cook, stirring, 2 to 3 minutes. Add drained barley and carrot; cook, stirring, 2 to 3 minutes. Stir in broth; cover and simmer 1 hour.

Meanwhile, cook pasta according to package directions. Drain well.

Add cauliflower and/or broccoli to soup; cook until vegetables are tender. Stir in cilantro and drained pasta; simmer 2 to 3 minutes. Serve immediately.

Maritime Bouillabaisse

Julie Watson
Cookbook Author, Charlottetown, Prince Edward Island, Canada

A favorite cold weather treat, this rich seafood stew is our choice after a skate or sleigh ride. We prepare the broth ahead of time to make for a quick nourishing meal. Bouillabaisse adapts perfectly to fish and shellfish available in any region of the world. The secrets are a tasty broth and being careful to not overcook the seafood.

Makes 8 servings

¼ cup vegetable oil
3 medium onions, chopped
3 cloves garlic, crushed
6 cups cold water
3 cups canned or fresh peeled and chopped tomatoes
2 teaspoons salt
½ teaspoon black pepper
¼ teaspoon dried savory
¼ teaspoon saffron
1 tablespoon chopped fresh parsley

¼ teaspoon dried thyme
1 bay leaf
3 ounces shell macaroni or spiral pasta (1¼ cups)
2 pounds fish fillets (1 pound each of 2 varieties)
¼ cup lemon juice
1 pound blue mussels, in the shell
2 cooked lobsters or crabs, in the shell
Toast or French bread

Heat oil in a large saucepan or Dutch oven. Add onions and garlic; cook, stirring, over low heat until onions are tender. Add water, tomatoes, salt, pepper, savory, saffron, parsley, thyme and bay leaf; mix well. Heat to boiling. Reduce heat; simmer until ready to add seafood.

Meanwhile, cook pasta according to package directions. Drain well.

Cut fish into 8 to 12 serving-size chunks. Add fish and lemon juice to broth. Simmer, covered, 5 minutes. Add mussels; simmer 5 minutes, or until fish almost flakes.

Chop cooked lobster or crab into pieces. Add pasta and lobster to broth. Simmer a few minutes, until all ingredients are hot. The mussels should be fully open; discard any whose shells remain closed. Taste and adjust seasonings. Serve immediately with toast or French bread.

Note: To serve this soup, we usually leave everything in the cooking pot and place it right on the table. The informality of "digging in" makes

Ask bars, restaurants and arenas to sponsor Designated Driver programs.

for casual fun. Toast or bread is used to sop up the broth. For a more formal presentation, strain the broth into a warm soup tureen; arrange cooked seafood on a heated platter. To serve, ladle broth into soup plates, each containing a triangle of toast or crisp French bread. Add equal portions of fish and seafood to each serving.

Pasta and Bean Soup

Cynthia David
Food Editor, *Toronto Sun*, Toronto, Ontario, Canada

This thick 'n' hearty soup proves that healthful eating doesn't have to be expensive. It also proves how easy cooking can be with a few staples, such as canned tomatoes and kidney beans, on hand. Sausage is another useful ingredient – so flavorful you hardly need to add any other spices. Make up a big batch of this soup and store it in the freezer for extra-busy nights.

Makes 4 to 6 servings

8 ounces elbow macaroni (2 cups)
1 pound mild or hot Italian
   sausage, casing removed
1 large onion, chopped
2 medium carrots, finely chopped
1 clove garlic, finely chopped
1 (28-ounce) can whole tomatoes,
   undrained

2 cups chicken broth
1 teaspoon dried basil
1 teaspoon dried rosemary
1 teaspoon dried oregano
1 (19-ounce) can kidney beans,
   drained and rinsed
2 tablespoons grated
   Parmesan cheese

Cook pasta al dente according to package directions. Drain well.

Meanwhile, cook sausage in a large saucepan over medium heat about 5 minutes, or until brown. Drain fat. Add onion, carrots and garlic; cook, stirring, 6 minutes, or until carrots are tender.

Break up tomatoes with a fork or knife. Add tomatoes with their liquid, broth, basil, rosemary and oregano to sausage mixture. Bring to boiling. Add beans and cooked pasta; mix gently. Simmer 2 minutes. Spoon into soup bowls; garnish each serving with Parmesan cheese.

Pasta Salad with Roasted Tomatoes

Jeanne Voltz
Cookbook Author, Pittsboro, NC

Every color of the garden is represented here: red tomatoes; green, golden and purple bell peppers; the creamy green of avocado; and crisp green lettuce for framing the riot of color you've assembled. The tomatoes are smoked or oven-roasted to bring out their maximum flavor.

Makes 4 to 5 servings

Juice of 1/2 lime
  (about 1 tablespoon)
1/2 cup cubed avocado
2 large tomatoes or 6 to 10 plum
  (Roma) tomatoes
  (about 1 pound)
1/2 teaspoon crushed red pepper,
  or to taste
1 clove garlic, finely chopped
1/2 cup peeled and chopped
  cucumber
1/4 cup chopped green bell pepper

1/4 cup chopped purple bell pepper
1/4 cup chopped yellow bell pepper
1/4 cup chopped sweet onion
1/4 cup sliced green onions
  (green part only)
3 tablespoons olive oil, divided
Salt
8 ounces pasta wheels or
  spiral pasta (3 cups)
Lettuce leaves, for garnish

Sprinkle lime juice on avocado to prevent darkening; set aside.

Rinse tomatoes, then cut in half vertically. Place halves, cut-side down, on an oiled rack in a shallow baking pan. Place pan on grid over hot coals in a grill or in a preheated 300° oven. Grill or roast 30 to 45 minutes, or until tomatoes are soft.

Peel roasted tomatoes; discard skins. Puree tomato pulp in a food processor or mash with a fork or spoon in a bowl.

In a large serving bowl, combine tomato puree, red pepper flakes, garlic, cucumber, bell peppers, onion and green onions. Stir in 1 tablespoon of the olive oil; mix well. Season to taste with salt. Add avocado mixture; mix lightly. Let stand at room temperature 1 to 2 hours to allow flavors to blend.

Select a Designated Driver when your outing will involve alcohol.

Cook pasta al dente according to package directions. Drain well. Drizzle remaining 2 tablespoons olive oil over pasta; mix. Add pasta to tomato mixture; mix gently. Tuck lettuce leaves around the rim of the bowl. Serve immediately.

Ramen Vegetable Salad

Beth W. Orenstein
Free-Lance Writer, Northampton, PA

This is my younger sister's contribution to our family get-togethers throughout the summer. My 5-year-old twin daughters can't get enough of it. Its mild flavor makes it an ideal accompaniment to any main course prepared on the grill.

Makes 6 to 8 servings

2 (3-ounce) packages instant ramen noodles (any flavor)
1 (8-ounce) can sliced water chestnuts, drained and rinsed
1 large green bell pepper, chopped
5 to 7 green onions, sliced
1 large tomato, chopped
1/4 cup olive oil
2 teaspoons red wine vinegar
Salt and black pepper
Chopped fresh parsley

Remove seasoning packets from noodles; discard or save for another use. Cook noodles according to package directions (except do not add the seasoning packets). Drain noodles, then rinse with cold water. Drain well.

In a large serving bowl, combine noodles, water chestnuts, bell pepper, green onions and tomato; mix well.

In a small bowl, combine olive oil and vinegar; stir or whisk to mix well. Pour oil mixture over noodle mixture; mix gently to coat all ingredients. Season to taste with salt and pepper. Garnish with parsley. Refrigerate, covered, until serving time.

Shrimp and Macaroni Salad

Suzanne Hall
Food Editor, *The Chattanooga Times*, Chattanooga, TN

Periodically I ask readers to send me their favorite recipes. I rarely get duplications and can always count on getting several to add to my personal list of favorites. This is one of them. When served with warm bread and fresh fruit for dessert, it's a luncheon or supper meal-in-one with a wide variety of flavors. Because you can buy frozen cooked and peeled shrimp at the supermarket, this recipe is quite simple to prepare.

Makes 6 to 8 servings

4 ounces elbow macaroni (1 cup)
1 1/2 pounds frozen cooked and peeled small shrimp, thawed
1 cup frozen peas, thawed (not necessary to cook)
2 hard-cooked eggs, peeled and chopped
1 green bell pepper, chopped
1/4 cup chopped green olives
2 tablespoons chopped pimento
1 tablespoon chopped onion
1 cup mayonnaise
1/2 teaspoon salt
1/8 teaspoon black pepper
Lettuce leaves

Cook macaroni according to package directions. Drain well.

In a large serving bowl, combine macaroni, shrimp, peas, eggs, bell pepper, olives, pimento and onion; mix gently.

In a small bowl, combine mayonnaise, salt and pepper; stir to mix. Pour over pasta mixture; mix gently to coat all ingredients. Refrigerate, covered, at least 2 hours, or overnight. Serve on lettuce leaves.

Never let anyone drink and drive.

Stir-Fry Salad

Toni Burks
Free-Lance Writer, Roanoke, VA

Orzo is a small pasta shape that bears a striking resemblance to plump rice kernels. Indeed, it is a delicious substitute for rice in main-dish salads. Orzo requires a few more minutes to cook than some pastas, so you can put it on to cook while you slice and dice the other ingredients.

Makes 4 servings

2 ounces orzo (1/2 cup)
1/3 cup water
2 tablespoons soy sauce
1 1/2 tablespoons distilled white vinegar
1 tablespoon cornstarch
1/2 teaspoon granulated sugar
1 1/2 tablespoons vegetable oil
8 ounces skinned, boned chicken breast, cut into bite-size pieces

8 ounces fresh mushrooms, stems trimmed
4 ounces fresh green beans, trimmed and cut into thirds
1 tablespoon finely chopped garlic
1 tablespoon finely chopped fresh ginger
3/4 cup cherry tomato halves
Lettuce leaves

Cook orzo according to package directions. Drain well. Keep warm.

Meanwhile, in a small bowl, combine water, soy sauce, vinegar, cornstarch and sugar; mix well. Set aside.

Heat oil in a large skillet or wok. Add chicken, mushrooms, beans, garlic and ginger; cook, stirring, over high heat 5 to 6 minutes, or until chicken is done. Add tomatoes; cook, stirring, 1 minute. Reduce heat to low. Stir reserved soy sauce mixture; pour over chicken mixture in skillet. Cook, stirring gently, 2 minutes, or until sauce thickens slightly. Stir in orzo.

Line serving plates with lettuce. Spoon hot salad mixture onto lettuce. Serve immediately.

Note: Substitute 8 ounces peeled shrimp for chicken, if desired. Cook mushrooms, beans, garlic and ginger in oil about 5 minutes, then add shrimp and cook, stirring, 1 minute. Add tomatoes and continue with the recipe.

Tomato-Cheese Pasta Salad

Constance Hay
Free-Lance Food Writer, Columbia, MD

It's summertime and the fresh tomatoes are bursting with flavor, but you've run out of ways to use them. Hurry out to the garden or produce stand and try this refreshing pasta salad. Serve it with a loaf of crunchy bread for a quick luncheon entree on a hot day.

Makes 4 servings

8 ounces shell macaroni (3 cups)
8 ounces mozzarella cheese, cubed (about 2 cups)
2 tomatoes, peeled and cut into small wedges
1 cup sliced cooked ham
1/4 cup sliced ripe olives
1/3 cup bottled olive oil and vinegar salad dressing
2 tablespoons chopped fresh basil
Lettuce leaves

Cook pasta *al dente* according to package directions. Drain, then rinse with cold water to cool quickly. Drain well.

In a large bowl, combine pasta, cheese, tomatoes, ham, olives, salad dressing and basil; mix to coat ingredients. Refrigerate, covered, until serving time. Serve on lettuce.

Support your local MADD chapter.

Tortellini Soup

Lori Longbotham
Free-Lance Food Writer, New York, NY

This just might be the quickest, easiest and freshest soup that you can make. If you keep refrigerated tortellini on hand or pick some up on the way home from work along with watercress and green onions, you can have soup for lunch, dinner or a snack in minutes.

Makes 4 servings

8 ounces refrigerated meat or cheese tortellini (2 cups)
2 (13 3/4-ounce) cans chicken broth
1 bunch watercress
1/4 cup finely chopped green onions
4 tablespoons grated Parmesan cheese, divided
1/4 teaspoon crushed red pepper

Cook tortellini according to package directions. Drain well.

Meanwhile, heat broth to boiling in a medium saucepan. Discard large stems of watercress; cut small stems crosswise into thirds. Stir tortellini, watercress, green onions, 2 tablespoons of the Parmesan cheese and red pepper flakes into broth. Cook over medium-high heat 2 minutes.

Sprinkle each serving with about 1/2 tablespoon (1 1/2 teaspoons) of the remaining Parmesan cheese. Serve immediately.

Tortellini Vegetable Salad

Alice Handkins
Free-Lance Food Writer, Wichita, KS

This colorful, nutritious salad combines tortellini with carrots, broccoli, artichoke hearts, ripe olives and feta cheese. It is a welcome menu addition to picnics, barbecues and church dinners. Individual servings look pretty on lettuce-lined plates. This salad makes a satisfying main dish when served with crisp bread sticks or crusty Italian bread.

Makes 8 servings

12 ounces refrigerated cheese tortellini (3 cups)

1 1/2 cups bottled Italian salad dressing

2 cups broccoli florets

3 carrots, sliced (about 2 cups)

1 (14-ounce) can artichoke hearts, drained and halved

1 (6-ounce) can ripe olives, drained and halved

1/4 cup chopped green bell pepper

1/2 medium cucumber, peeled and chopped

2 large tomatoes, peeled and chopped

1/2 cup crumbled feta cheese

3 green onions, chopped

1 tablespoon finely chopped fresh basil or 1 teaspoon dried

Cook tortellini according to package directions. Drain well. Put tortellini in a large serving bowl. Pour Italian dressing over tortellini; mix gently.

Blanch broccoli in boiling water about 15 seconds. Drain; add to pasta mixture.

Cook carrots in boiling water about 1 minute, or until tender-crisp. Drain carrots; add to pasta mixture.

Add artichoke hearts, olives, bell pepper, cucumber, tomatoes, feta cheese, green onions and basil to pasta mixture; mix gently. Refrigerate, covered, at least 1 hour, or until serving time. Stir again just before serving so all vegetables and pasta are coated with dressing.

Attend a MADD event and discover why your support is so important.

Fish *and* Seafood

Bow Ties with Salmon

Barbara Yost
Feature Writer, *The Phoenix Gazette*, Phoenix, AZ

This is a fast and easy dish using fun-shaped pasta. I once prepared it for my father using football-shaped pasta. It's also a good way to sneak spinach past the kids. They'll love this dish as much as you do. I also like it because I can use fresh lemons from the lemon tree in my backyard. I usually add a little extra juice for a bit more zip. The citrus flavor goes great with the salmon.

Makes 4 servings

1 cup heavy cream
2 tablespoons fresh lemon juice
1 teaspoon salt
1/4 teaspoon black pepper
1/4 teaspoon dried dill weed
  or 3/4 teaspoon fresh dill
1 pound fresh spinach, trimmed
  and cut into fine shreds

1 pound boned and skinned
  salmon, cut into bite-size
  pieces
6 ounces bow tie pasta (3 cups)
2 hard-cooked eggs, peeled and
  crumbled

In a heavy skillet, combine cream, lemon juice, salt, pepper and dill weed. Bring to a simmer over medium heat. Add spinach; cook 1 minute, stirring constantly, or until spinach is wilted. Add salmon; cook, stirring gently, about 2 minutes.

Meanwhile, cook pasta according to package directions. Drain well. Put pasta in a large serving bowl. Pour salmon sauce over pasta; mix gently. Sprinkle egg over top. Serve immediately.

MADD needs your help to stop the problem of drinking and driving.

Fettuccine with Scallops

Lori Longbotham
Free-Lance Food Writer, New York, NY

You'll love this recipe because it's so quick that it gives you some time to yourself (even though your family will think you slaved all day in the kitchen). Your family will love it because it's delicious and unusual. If you've been looking for something new for your meal plans, this is it.

Makes 4 servings

2 tablespoons butter
1 sweet onion, quartered
    lengthwise and sliced thin
3 cups chopped peeled tomatoes
Peel of 1 orange, removed in
    strips with a vegetable peeler
3 tablespoons chicken broth

1/2 teaspoon dried rosemary
1/2 teaspoon dried basil
Dash freshly ground black pepper
16 ounces fettuccine
8 ounces bay scallops, rinsed
Chopped fresh parsley

Melt butter in a large heavy skillet over medium heat. Add onion; cook, stirring occasionally, 5 minutes, or until softened. Stir in tomatoes, orange peel, broth, rosemary, basil and pepper. Cook, covered, 5 minutes.

Meanwhile, cook pasta *al dente* according to package directions. Drain well.

Stir scallops into sauce. Cook over medium heat, stirring frequently, 2 minutes, or until scallops are opaque. Remove and discard orange peel.

Transfer cooked pasta to a warmed serving bowl. Pour scallops and sauce over pasta. Garnish with parsley. Serve immediately.

Linguine with Clam Sauce

Caroline Stuart
Cookbook Author, Greenwich, CT

You'll find linguine with clam sauce on most Italian restaurant menus, which attests to its popularity. However, it's quite simple to prepare at home because the ingredients are readily available. This recipe calls for chopped canned clams, but small, whole canned clams work well, as do fresh clams with their juice.

Makes 4 servings

16 ounces linguine
¼ cup olive oil
2 cloves garlic, finely chopped
¼ cup butter
1 tablespoon chopped fresh parsley

1 (8-ounce) can chopped clams, undrained
Salt and freshly ground black pepper
Grated Romano or Parmesan cheese

Cook linguine according to package directions. Drain well.

Heat olive oil in a saucepan. Add garlic; cook, stirring, over medium-low heat until soft but not brown. Stir in butter. When butter has melted, add parsley and clams with their liquid. Simmer 10 to 15 minutes. Season to taste with salt and pepper.

Transfer pasta to a warmed pasta bowl; pour clam sauce over pasta. Garnish with cheese. Serve immediately.

Ask your friends and family to pledge to be safe and sober drivers.

Low-Fat Fresh Mussel Pasta

Susan Manlin Katzman
Free-Lance Food Writer, St. Louis, MO

Sarah is my recently-graduated-from-college daughter who has moved back home until she can save enough money to move to Los Angeles and make films along with Steven and Woody. The goal of starting out big in Hollywood might strike terror in the minds of some moms, but I believe in Sarah. She is very clever. Look at her now. She has a rent-free home (with swimming pool and laundry privileges). And she has a private cook — I make her dinners. But that's not all. It's what she has me cooking that's important. Sarah's most-requested dish is fresh mussel pasta, a delicious, almost fat-free entree. I ask you, could you ever doubt that a kid who could arrange this sweet life at 21 is headed for success?

Makes 4 to 6 servings

2 pounds fresh mussels, cleaned and ready to cook
1 (28-ounce) can crushed tomatoes
2 cups chicken broth
1 large onion, finely chopped
2 ribs celery, finely chopped
2 large cloves garlic, finely chopped
1 teaspoon dried oregano
1 teaspoon dried thyme
Salt and black pepper, to taste
12 ounces spiral pasta (4 1/2 cups)
Grated Parmesan cheese (optional)

Cook mussels and pasta so that both are done at the same time.

Start by bringing a large pot of water (for the pasta) to a full rolling boil. While the pasta water is coming to a boil, put mussels, tomatoes, broth, onion, celery, garlic, oregano, thyme, salt and pepper in a small stockpot. Cover and bring mixture to boiling over high heat. Boil 10 to 15 minutes, stirring once halfway through cooking, or until mussels are open. (Discard all mussels that do not open when others are fully open.)

While mussels are cooking, add pasta to boiling water and cook *al dente* according to package directions. Drain pasta.

Add cooked pasta to mussel mixture; stir well. Serve immediately with Parmesan cheese, if desired.

Pasta Escargot

Zack Hanle
Editor-at-Large, *Bon Appétit*, New York, NY

> *Having been gifted by a favorite daughter-in-law with several dozen cans of escargot and having some guests who professed not to like snails, I tried this combination one evening with instant acclaim. The dish takes mere minutes to prepare and is best served with French bread and a tossed green salad. I told my guests it was simply "pasta with a French twist."*

Makes 4 servings

4 tablespoons butter, softened
4 large cloves garlic,
   finely chopped
2 tablespoons finely chopped
   fresh parsley
Dash ground nutmeg
Dash freshly ground black pepper

Dash salt
8 ounces angel hair pasta
2 (4 1/2-ounce) cans snails
   (24 giant size) or
   1 (7 1/2-ounce) can snails
   (36 small), drained

In a small bowl, combine butter, garlic, parsley, nutmeg, pepper and salt; mix well.

Cook pasta according to package directions. Drain well. Divide pasta among 4 serving plates or bowls. Spoon one-fourth of the butter mixture on top of each serving; mix until butter melts. Add one-fourth of the snails to each serving; mix again. Serve immediately.

Be a responsible host.

Pasta with Smoked Salmon

Narcisse S. Cadgène
Free-Lance Writer, New York, NY

Silky, creamy, smoky, sensuous and sensational, this dish is not to be missed. Often the expense of smoked salmon can be cut substantially by asking the deli for the bits and pieces, which are typically sold at a reduced price. Even at top dollar, though, this recipe is worth it.

Makes 2 servings

1 tablespoon butter or olive oil (preferably extra virgin)	1 tablespoon chopped fresh basil
1 clove garlic, finely chopped	2 to 4 ounces smoked salmon, chopped
3 tablespoons finely chopped red onion	1/4 cup heavy cream
1 tablespoon chopped fresh parsley	8 ounces fresh pasta, such as fettuccine, linguine or spaghetti
1 tablespoon finely chopped green onion	Freshly ground black pepper

Melt butter in a saucepan over medium heat. Stir in garlic and red onion. Cook, stirring, 1 to 2 minutes, or until vegetables just begin to soften. Add parsley, green onion, basil and salmon; cook just until heated through. Add cream; heat until the cream is quite warm, but do not boil. Remove from heat.

Meanwhile, cook pasta *al dente* according to package directions. Do not overcook. Drain well.

Mix hot cooked pasta with warm salmon sauce. Divide mixture between 2 serving plates. Top each serving with freshly ground black pepper.

Never serve alcohol to anyone who has had too much to drink. 81

Penne with Shrimp and Roasted Peppers

Lori Longbotham
Free-Lance Food Writer, New York, NY

I love when the fragrance of roasting peppers fills my kitchen. To me it's the most alluring and tantalizing of food smells --wonderfully earthy. So try this dish and fill your kitchen with the lovely aroma. Peppers also can be roasted on a charcoal grill, directly over a gas flame, or even on a rack over an electric burner. Any of these methods will produce perfectly roasted peppers and a fragrant kitchen.

Makes 2 servings

1 medium-size red bell pepper
1 medium-size yellow bell pepper
1/2 cup chicken broth, divided
1 teaspoon vegetable oil
2 small onions, thinly sliced
2 small leeks (white part only), thinly sliced
1 teaspoon finely chopped garlic
6 shiitake mushrooms (2 ounces), stems discarded, sliced thin (or substitute button mushrooms)
2 sun-dried tomatoes packed in oil, drained and chopped
1 tablespoon finely chopped fresh parsley

1 teaspoon capers, drained
1/2 teaspoon finely chopped fresh oregano leaves or a dash of dried
1/2 teaspoon balsamic or red wine vinegar
1/4 teaspoon freshly ground black pepper, or to taste
Salt, to taste
10 ounces cooked medium shrimp, peeled and deveined
5 ounces penne (1 1/4 cups)
2 tablespoons freshly grated Parmesan cheese, divided

Broil peppers 4 inches from heat for 15 to 20 minutes, turning as needed to blacken on all sides. Place peppers in a large bowl; cover bowl with a plate and let peppers steam a few minutes. Remove the skins of the peppers with a paring knife, then remove stems. Cut peppers in half and scrape out seeds and ribs; reserve juices in a large bowl. Cut peppers into 1/2-inch pieces; add to reserved juices in bowl.

Meanwhile, heat 1/4 cup of the broth and oil in a medium nonstick skillet over medium heat. Add onions and leeks; cook, stirring occasionally, 10 minutes, or until light brown. Add garlic and cook, stirring

Stop serving drinks at least 90 minutes before the party ends.

constantly, 5 minutes. Add onion mixture to peppers in bowl.

Heat remaining 1/4 cup broth in same skillet over medium heat. Add mushrooms; cook, stirring occasionally, 3 to 5 minutes, or until softened and broth has almost completely evaporated. Add mushrooms to vegetable mixture in bowl. Add tomatoes, parsley, capers, oregano, vinegar, pepper, salt and shrimp; mix well.

Meanwhile, cook pasta *al dente* according to package directions. Drain well. Put pasta on a large serving platter. Sprinkle 1 tablespoon of the Parmesan cheese on pasta; stir to mix. Pour roasted pepper sauce over pasta; mix gently. Divide pasta mixture evenly between 2 plates. Sprinkle with remaining 1 tablespoon Parmesan cheese. Serve immediately.

Note: This recipe easily can be doubled or tripled.

Shrimp Spaghetti

Ann Hattes
Free-Lance Writer, Hartland, WI

This recipe, easily prepared at the last minute, can be served to guests as well as the family. It is a meal by itself, or can be dressed up with a salad and light dessert. I use frozen precooked small shrimp, which work well in this recipe. With enough shrimp in the freezer and pasta on hand, this recipe can be prepared quickly for almost any number of unexpected drop-in supper guests. I haven't found anyone yet who doesn't like it.

Makes 4 servings

8 ounces spaghetti	1/3 cup grated Parmesan cheese
1/3 cup olive oil	1/4 cup chopped fresh dill or
2 (6-ounce) packages frozen	1 tablespoon dried dill weed
cooked and peeled shrimp,	1 teaspoon salt
partly thawed and drained	1/2 teaspoon black pepper

Cook spaghetti according to package directions. Drain.

Meanwhile, heat olive oil in a large skillet. Add shrimp; cook, stirring, 1 to 2 minutes. Stir in cooked spaghetti, Parmesan cheese, dill, salt and pepper. Toss or stir to coat all ingredients. Serve immediately.

Don't serve alcohol to guests who have already had too much to drink. 83

Shrimp Vermicelli Casserole

Eleanor Ostman
Food Writer, *St. Paul Pioneer Press*, St. Paul, MN

It took a bit of prying, but I finally got this recipe from Mrs. Harry Given, the wife of St. Paul's premier caterer, who in turn got it from a friend. Considering the price of shrimp, I discovered that cutting them in half lengthwise while cleaning them greatly increases their presence among the strands of vermicelli. Be sure the pasta is undercooked before putting it in the casserole for further baking, or it might become mushy.

Makes 6 to 8 servings

1/2 cup butter, divided
1 cup thinly sliced green onions
5 tablespoons all-purpose flour
2 1/2 cups chicken broth
1/2 cup clam juice
1/2 cup heavy cream
1/2 teaspoon dried oregano

1/2 cup grated Parmesan cheese, divided
2 cloves garlic
1/2 pound fresh mushrooms, sliced
4 ounces vermicelli (thin spaghetti)
4 cups cooked and peeled extra-large shrimp

Melt 1/4 cup of the butter in a large skillet. Add green onions; cook, stirring, until soft. Mix in flour; stir until smooth. Add broth, clam juice, cream and oregano; stir until well blended. Simmer 3 minutes. Stir in 1/4 cup of the Parmesan cheese.

Melt remaining 1/4 cup butter in another skillet. Add whole garlic cloves and sliced mushrooms. Cook quickly; remove and discard garlic.

Cook vermicelli *al dente* according to package directions. Drain well.

Combine cooked pasta with sauce, mushroom mixture and shrimp; mix gently. Spoon into a lightly greased 13x9x2-inch baking pan. Top with remaining 1/4 cup Parmesan cheese.

Bake, uncovered, in a preheated 375° oven 30 minutes, or until bubbly.

Note: You can extend the casserole somewhat by increasing the amount of pasta, up to 8 ounces.

Be a responsible guest. Don't drink to excess at your host's home.

Tortellini Bari

Jim Hillibish
City Editor, *The Repository*, Canton, OH

Bari is a city in southeastern Italy on the Adriatic Sea known for excellent prosciutto hams. The dry, pressed meat, always eaten in small amounts, is more of a flavoring condiment than a main course. This tortellini main dish uses the salty flavoring of prosciutto to complement the thick, tasty prawns found off the Italian coast. Prosciutto is found in Italian markets.

Makes 6 servings

20 ounces refrigerated ricotta cheese tortellini (5 cups)
1 pound prawns or shrimp, peeled and deveined
2 cups heavy cream
1 teaspoon freshly grated nutmeg
1/4 teaspoon cayenne pepper
3/4 cup fresh or frozen baby peas
1/2 cup freshly grated Parmesan cheese
1 1/2 ounces prosciutto, thinly sliced
Salt and freshly ground black pepper

Cook tortellini *al dente* according to package directions, adding prawns during the last 2 minutes of cooking. Drain well.

Meanwhile, bring cream just to boiling in a heavy saucepan. Reduce heat. Stir in nutmeg and cayenne. Simmer, stirring, until slightly thickened.

Return tortellini and prawns to their cooking pot. Add warm cream mixture, peas, Parmesan cheese and prosciutto; mix gently. Simmer over low heat about 3 minutes, stirring occasionally, until prawns are done, tortellini are tender and sauce thickens. Season to taste with salt and pepper. Serve immediately.

Tuna-Pepper Penne

Cynthia David
Food Editor, *Toronto Sun*, Toronto, Ontario, Canada

Solve the what's-for-dinner dilemma with this spicy, exotic-flavored recipe made with ordinary items. Capers are the secret ingredient – they're sun-dried flower buds from a Mediterranean bush, preserved in a vinegar brine. While the pasta is cooking, soften the bell pepper strips and stir in the tuna and tomato sauce. By the time the pasta is cooked and drained, the sauce will be ready to go.

Makes 2 servings

8 ounces penne (2 cups)
3 tablespoons olive oil
2 green or red bell peppers, sliced
    into thin strips
1 large clove garlic, finely chopped
2 teaspoons chopped fresh parsley
2 teaspoons capers, drained

Dash crushed red pepper
1 (6-ounce) can water-packed tuna,
    drained and flaked
1/2 cup tomato sauce
Salt and black pepper
1/4 cup chopped fresh basil

Cook pasta according to package directions. Drain well.

Meanwhile, heat olive oil in a large skillet over medium-high heat. Add bell pepper strips; cook, stirring frequently, 10 minutes, or until tender-crisp and light brown. Add garlic, parsley, capers and red pepper flakes. Cook, stirring constantly, 1 to 2 minutes. Stir in tuna, then tomato sauce. Heat through. Season to taste with salt and pepper.

Add cooked pasta and basil to sauce; mix gently. Serve immediately.

Remember to Drive Smart and Drive Sober.

Meats *and* Poultry

Baked Ziti

Jeanne Voltz
Cookbook Author, Pittsboro, NC

The garlicky tomato sauce with Italian sausage gives a Neapolitan flavor to this casserole, which is a regular at church suppers in northeastern New Jersey. Ziti, a tubular pasta about ¼ inch in diameter and two inches long, is available in most supermarkets. If you don't find ziti, use penne or another similar shape; even elbow macaroni is okay.

Makes 6 to 8 servings

½ pound Italian sausage, sweet or hot, cut in ½-inch slices
½ pound lean ground beef or veal
4 to 5 cups meatless tomato sauce for pasta (homemade or store-bought)
1 cup chicken broth
1½ teaspoons dried oregano
Salt and black pepper

8 ounces ziti or other tubular macaroni (2 cups)
1 egg
1 cup ricotta cheese
⅓ cup finely chopped fresh parsley or 2 tablespoons dried
2 cups shredded mozzarella cheese (8 ounces)
½ cup grated Parmesan cheese

Put sliced sausage in a large skillet; cook, stirring frequently, until brown. Transfer to a plate and keep warm. Cook ground beef in sausage drippings in the same skillet until light brown; stir to keep meat crumbly. Return sausage to skillet. Stir in tomato sauce, broth and oregano; mix well. Season to taste with salt and pepper.

Cook ziti *al dente* according to package directions. Drain well.

In a small bowl, combine egg, ricotta cheese and parsley; mix well.

Ladle a large spoonful of sauce into a shallow 2-quart baking dish. Spread a large spoonful of the ricotta mixture in the sauce. Top with half of the cooked ziti, half the remaining sauce, half of the mozzarella cheese and the remaining ricotta mixture. Repeat layers of ziti, sauce and mozzarella. Sprinkle Parmesan cheese on top.

Bake in a preheated 350° oven 35 minutes, or until bubbly. Let cool 15 minutes on a wire rack; cut into rectangles to serve.

Learn the facts about the dangers of drinking and driving.

Caesar Pasta

Mary D. Scourtes
Food Writer, *The Tampa Tribune*, Tampa, FL

Everyone loves the flavor of Caesar salad, so why not combine the wonderful, rich taste of that dish with your favorite pasta? If you dislike anchovies, you can omit the anchovy paste in this recipe.

Makes 4 servings

16 ounces fettuccine
1/3 cup freshly grated Parmesan cheese
3 tablespoons butter, softened
2 teaspoons lemon juice
1 tablespoon Dijon-style mustard
1 teaspoon grated lemon peel

1 1/2 teaspoons anchovy paste
1 clove garlic, finely chopped
1/2 teaspoon hot pepper sauce
2 dashes Worcestershire sauce
1 pound beef sirloin steak, grilled and sliced into bite-size pieces
Freshly ground black pepper

Cook pasta according to package directions. Drain well.

In a large bowl, combine Parmesan cheese, butter, lemon juice, mustard, lemon peel, anchovy paste, garlic, hot pepper sauce and Worcestershire sauce; mix well. Add grilled steak and cooked pasta. Mix gently until all ingredients are well coated. Season to taste with pepper. Serve at once.

Note: Omit the steak and serve the pasta as a side dish or first course.

Chicken and Vegetable Pasta Supper

Susan Manlin Katzman
Free-Lance Food Writer, St. Louis, MO

I once interviewed Tony Bommarito, who at the time owned my favorite restaurant, the elegant and pricey Anthony's in St. Louis. When I asked him what owners/chefs of famous restaurants serve at home for family meals, Tony said he liked to roast chicken on a bed of vegetables and toss the pan juices with pasta. Tony's dish sounded so good, I tried it that very night and have made it ever since. Many years later, I told Tony how his recipe had become a Katzman family mainstay. "What?" he said. "I don't remember any dish like that." Well, whoever is responsible, I like the dish and believe you will, too. The recipe is adjustable, and you can make it your own by varying the vegetables and the pasta shapes.

Makes 4 servings

About 4 cups cut-up vegetables (carrots, celery, zucchini, sweet potatoes, turnips, acorn squash, yellow squash, parsnips, etc.)

1 medium-size yellow onion, cut into bite-size pieces

1/4 cup olive oil

About 1 tablespoon Dijon-style mustard

2 large cloves garlic, finely chopped

1 teaspoon dried oregano

1/2 teaspoon dried thyme

1/2 teaspoon celery salt

Salt and coarsely ground black pepper, to taste

1 (2 1/2- to 3 1/2-pound) broiler-fryer chicken, cut into serving pieces

8 ounces pasta (spaghetti or any fancy shaped pasta such as bow ties, shell macaroni, wheels, etc.)

Olive oil (optional)

Freshly grated Parmesan cheese (optional)

Use at least 4 different kinds of vegetables. Peel and trim them as necessary and cut into bite-size pieces. Put prepared vegetables and onion in a 13x9x2-inch baking pan.

In a small bowl, combine 1/4 cup olive oil and mustard; mix well. Drizzle about 3 tablespoons of the mustard oil over vegetables. Sprinkle

Recognize the signs of the alcohol-impaired driver.

garlic, oregano, thyme, celery salt, salt and pepper over vegetables; stir gently to distribute seasonings.

Arrange chicken pieces, skin-side up, in one layer on top of vegetables. Brush remaining mustard oil on chicken. Season chcken with salt and pepper.

Bake, uncovered, in a preheated 350° oven about 1 hour, or until chicken is brown and cooked through and vegetables are tender.

About 15 minutes before chicken is done, cook pasta according to package directions. Drain well. Put pasta in a large serving bowl and keep warm.

Remove chicken from oven; place chicken on a serving platter and keep warm.

Add vegetables and pan juices to pasta; mix gently. Taste and adjust seasonings. Add more olive oil for flavoring, if desired. Sprinkle Parmesan cheese on pasta mixture. Serve at once, serving chicken and vegetable pasta separately.

Chicken Noodle Casserole

Leona Carlson
Food Writer (Retired), *Rockford Register Star*, Rockford, IL

This is one of those never-fail classics that is just too easy. How can anything so uncomplicated and effortless taste so good? Well, it does.

Makes 2 to 3 servings

4 ounces egg noodles (2 1/2 cups)
1 (10 3/4-ounce) can cream of
   chicken soup, undiluted
1/3 cup low-fat or nonfat
   sour cream
1/3 cup water

2 tablespoons chopped fresh
   parsley
2 tablespoons chopped canned
   pimentos
1 cup chopped cooked chicken or
   turkey

Cook noodles according to package directions. Drain well.

In a lightly greased 1½-quart baking dish, combine soup, sour cream, water, parsley and pimentos; mix well. Stir in chicken and cooked noodles.

Bake in a preheated 350° oven 30 minutes, or until hot and bubbly.

Daddy's Away Casserole

Terry Briggs
Copy Editor, *The Macon Telegraph*, Macon, GA

While my brother and I were growing up, my father's job often required him to travel. When he was away, my mother would make simple meals. This casserole was one of our favorites. I have since made it for my husband and he likes it, too. The beauty of it is that you can add all sorts of ingredients to it and change the flavor as desired. In the summer when we have an abundance of squash, tomatoes and zucchini, I sauté some and add them to the casserole before baking.

Makes 6 servings

8 ounces egg noodles (5 cups)
1 1/2 pounds lean ground beef
1 medium onion, finely chopped
1 green bell pepper, chopped
1 clove garlic, crushed
1 (15 1/4-ounce) can whole-kernel corn, drained
1 (14 1/2-ounce) can stewed tomatoes, undrained
1 (8-ounce) can tomato sauce
1 teaspoon dried oregano
Salt and black pepper, to taste
2 cups shredded Cheddar cheese (8 ounces)

Cook noodles according to package directions. Drain well.

Cook ground beef in a medium skillet until brown, stirring frequently. Add onion, bell pepper and garlic; cook, stirring, until onion is tender. Drain off fat, if desired.

Spoon beef mixture into a lightly greased 2-quart baking dish. Add corn, tomatoes with their liquid, tomato sauce, oregano, salt and pepper; mix well. Stir in cooked noodles.

Bake in a preheated 375° oven 30 minutes. Sprinkle cheese on top. Return to oven and bake 10 minutes, or until golden brown and bubbly.

Protect yourself from injury caused by drunk drivers. Always wear your seat belt.

Day-After Turkey Divan

Mary D. Scourtes
Food Writer, *The Tampa Tribune*, Tampa, FL

To put a spin on the day after Thanksgiving, invite a group of friends to bring their Turkey Day leftovers disguised in various casseroles, salads or soups. You can even give a silly prize for the person who has the most innovative leftover dish. My favorite day-after turkey recipe is this one. It's so tasty I sometimes cook turkey just to make this casserole.

Makes 10 servings

12 ounces linguine
1 bunch fresh broccoli
    (about 1 pound)
2 tablespoons olive oil
1 bunch green onions, trimmed
    and sliced
5 cloves garlic, finely chopped
24 sun-dried tomatoes packed in
    oil, drained and cut into slivers
4 cups coarsely chopped cooked
    turkey
3/4 cup crumbled blue cheese

5 eggs
1 1/2 cups half-and-half or
    light cream
1/4 cup finely chopped fresh basil
    leaves
1/2 teaspoon salt
1 1/2 teaspoons freshly ground
    black pepper
1/2 cup dry bread crumbs
2 tablespoons butter or margarine,
    melted

Cook pasta according to package directions. Drain well.

Trim broccoli; cut florets into bite-size pieces. Cook broccoli in a small amount of water until just barely tender. Drain.

Heat olive oil in a heavy skillet over medium-high heat. Add green onions and garlic; cook, stirring, 3 to 4 minutes, or until soft. Add sun-dried tomatoes; cook 1 minute.

In a large bowl, combine tomato mixture and cooked pasta. Stir in cooked broccoli, turkey and blue cheese.

In a medium bowl, mix eggs and half-and-half. Add basil, salt and pepper; mix well. Pour egg mixture over pasta mixture; mix well. Transfer to a lightly greased 13x9x2-inch baking pan. Combine bread crumbs and melted butter; sprinkle on top of casserole. Bake in a preheated 350° oven 45 minutes, or until golden brown and bubbly.

Fresh Spaghetti Sauce

Janice Okun
Food Editor, *Buffalo News*, Buffalo, NY

At the end of the summer when home-grown tomatoes are at their peak, this is one of the most popular recipes in western New York. The sauce follows the old Italian-American tradition of long cooking and has an intense tomato flavor. Many people make large quantities of the sauce, then freeze it in 6-cup batches. It tastes mighty good when the winter winds blow.

Makes 6 cups sauce; enough for 4 servings of spaghetti

8 ounces hot Italian sausage links	2 teaspoons salt, divided
8 medium tomatoes, peeled and cored	1/2 teaspoon granulated sugar
1 large onion	1 pound lean ground beef
1 clove garlic	1/2 cup dry bread crumbs
1 (6-ounce) can tomato paste	Dash black pepper
2 teaspoons dried oregano	1 cup chopped fresh mushrooms
	16 ounces spaghetti

Cut sausage into 1-inch pieces. Cook slowly, stirring occasionally, in a small skillet until brown; drain on paper towels.

Place tomatoes, onion and garlic in container of electric blender or food processor; blend or process just until onion is finely chopped.

In a 4-quart saucepan, combine tomato mixture, tomato paste, oregano, 1 teaspoon of the salt and sugar; mix well. Bring to boiling. Reduce heat; simmer, uncovered, about 30 minutes, stirring occasionally.

Meanwhile, combine ground beef, bread crumbs, pepper and the remaining 1 teaspoon salt. Form mixture into 1/2-inch meatballs. Add sausage and meatballs to simmering sauce (do not brown meatballs before adding to sauce). Simmer, covered, over low heat about 2 hours, stirring occasionally.

About 15 minutes before sauce is finished, stir mushrooms into sauce. Cook spaghetti according to package directions. Drain well. Serve sauce over hot spaghetti.

Use proper car restraint systems for children.

Grandma's Casserole

Eleanor Ostman
Food Writer, *St. Paul Pioneer Press*, St. Paul, MN

My mother, Ellen Ostman of Hibbing, Minn., a wonderful "plain" cook, was an avid recipe clipper, as attested to by the boxfuls I sorted through after her death. She and my dad spent their last three winters together in Fort Meyers, Fla., and while there she cut out this recipe. As soon as she got back to Minnesota, she made it for her family, and it became a favorite. It also became treasured by my readers when I shared it after she died, because it's quickly made and the noodles don't have to be precooked.

Makes 8 to 10 servings

2 tablespoons butter or margarine
1 cup chopped onion
1 green bell pepper, cut into strips
1 1/2 pounds lean ground beef
1 teaspoon seasoned salt
1/2 teaspoon black pepper
1 tablespoon granulated sugar

1 (28- to 32-ounce) can whole tomatoes, undrained
1 (15-ounce) can tomato sauce
2 cups water
8 ounces wide egg noodles (5 cups)
8 ounces mozzarella cheese, sliced

Melt butter in a large skillet. Add onion and bell pepper; cook 3 minutes, stirring occasionally. Add ground beef; cook, breaking it up with a spoon, until brown. Add seasoned salt, pepper and sugar. Stir in tomatoes with their liquid, tomato sauce and water. Heat mixture to boiling. Reduce heat; simmer 15 minutes.

In a greased 13x9x2-inch baking pan, alternate layers of the meat mixture and the uncooked noodles. Arrange mozzarella slices on top.

Cover pan with aluminum foil. Bake in a preheated 350° oven 45 minutes, or until hot and bubbly. Cut into squares to serve.

Lazy Man's Pierogi

Janice Okun
Food Editor, *Buffalo News*, Buffalo, NY

Many Polish-Americans live in Buffalo and just about all of them love pierogi, half-moon-shaped dumplings that often are filled with mushrooms and sauerkraut. Pierogi, however, are time consuming to prepare. This is the easy version, served at parties because it can be prepared in advance, refrigerated and then heated just before serving time. It's also good for family meals, as a side dish or as the centerpiece of a light meal.

Makes 8 to 10 servings

½ pound bacon
1 cup chopped fresh mushrooms
2 onions, chopped
1 (16-ounce) can sauerkraut, drained

16 ounces spiral pasta (6 cups)
2 (10 ¾-ounce) cans cream of mushroom soup, undiluted
Salt and black pepper

Cut bacon into small pieces. Cook in a large skillet until crisp. Remove bacon from skillet; drain on paper towels.

Add mushrooms and onions to bacon drippings in the skillet; cook, stirring, until light brown. Remove mushroom mixture; drain well.

Rinse sauerkraut under cold water; drain well.

Cook macaroni according to package directions. Drain well.

In a large bowl, combine bacon, mushroom-onion mixture, sauerkraut and soup; mix well. Gently stir in cooked macaroni. Season to taste with salt and pepper.

Spoon mixture into a lightly greased 2-quart baking dish. Bake, uncovered, in a preheated 350° oven 30 minutes, or until mixture is hot and bubbly. Serve immediately.

Approximately 50% of all drivers killed in crashes between 6p.m. and 6a.m. had BAC of .10 or higher.

Make It Quick, I'm Hungry

Arlette Camp Copeland
Food Writer, *The Macon Telegraph*, Macon, GA

I have three busy children and a full-time job outside the home. Combine that with my husband's alternating schedule, and we often need something hearty for dinner in a flash. This is a zippy recipe a teen can learn to prepare and have ready when everyone arrives home. We like to use primavera sauce, but spaghetti sauce is good, too. The meatballs can be heated in the microwave oven, if you like. Serve the meatballs and pasta with toasted bread smeared with butter and sprinkled with garlic salt and dried parsley.

Makes 8 to 10 servings

3 tablespoons vegetable oil
1 (3-pound) bag frozen Italian
   meatballs, thawed

1 (32-ounce) jar primavera sauce
   or spaghetti sauce
16 ounces spinach linguine

Heat oil in a Dutch oven. Add meatballs; cook, stirring, until brown on all sides. Add sauce. Let simmer, stirring occasionally, while you cook the pasta.

Cook linguine according to package directions. Drain.

Serve meatballs and sauce over hot pasta.

Mexican Stuffed Shells

Jim Hillibish
City Editor, *The Repository*, Canton, OH

Pasta readily assumes the flavors of a sharp, spicy sauce. Mexican cuisine is the home of such sauces. This main dish is substantial enough to stand on its own with only a salad of fresh greens and some fruit to complete the meal. This recipe freezes well and can be reheated in the microwave oven.

Makes 4 servings

12 jumbo pasta shells	1/4 teaspoon ground cumin
1 pound lean ground beef	1/8 teaspoon chili powder
1 1/2 cups picante sauce (mild or medium, to taste)	1 (4-ounce) can chopped green chilies, drained
1 (8-ounce) can tomato sauce	1 1/2 cups shredded Monterey Jack cheese (6 ounces), divided
1/2 cup chicken broth	

Cook pasta shells according to package directions. Drain well.

Cook ground beef in a skillet, stirring occasionally to break up meat, until brown. Drain off fat.

In a medium bowl, combine picante sauce, tomato sauce, broth, cumin and chili powder; mix well.

Add 1/2 cup of the sauce mixture, chilies and 1/2 cup of the cheese to beef; mix well.

Spread half of the remaining sauce mixture in a 10-inch round baking dish. Stuff cooked pasta shells with beef mixture. Arrange shells in baking dish. Pour remaining sauce mixture over shells.

Bake, covered, in a preheated 350° oven 30 minutes, or until heated through. Top with remaining 1 cup cheese. Return to oven and bake, uncovered, 5 minutes, or until cheese is melted.

Alcohol involvement is highest in single-vehicle crashes weekdays between 6 p.m. - 6 a.m.

Million Dollar Spaghetti

Stacy Lam
Reporter, *The Macon Telegraph*, Macon, GA

I'm not sure where the expensive name came from, but I do know that this is the best baked spaghetti recipe I've tried. It's almost like lasagna with all the cheese, but it's easier to prepare. It's a great recipe to make ahead and freeze to bake later, or to bake and then freeze single-serving portions to reheat when needed.

Makes 6 servings

7 ounces thin spaghetti
1 1/2 pounds lean ground beef
2 (8-ounce) cans tomato sauce
1/2 teaspoon salt
1/4 teaspoon black pepper
1 (8-ounce) package cream cheese, softened
1 (8-ounce) carton cottage cheese
1/4 cup sour cream
1/3 cup chopped onion
1 tablespoon finely chopped green bell pepper
2 tablespoons butter or margarine, melted

Cook spaghetti according to package directions. Drain well.

Cook ground beef in a large skillet, stirring occasionally to break up meat, until brown. Drain off fat, if desired. Add tomato sauce, salt and pepper; mix well. Remove from heat.

In a medium bowl, combine cream cheese, cottage cheese, sour cream, onion and bell pepper; mix well.

Place half of the spaghetti in a lightly greased 2-quart baking dish. Spread cheese mixture on top of spaghetti. Place remaining spaghetti over cheese mixture. Pour melted butter over spaghetti. Top with beef mixture.

Bake, uncovered, in a preheated 350° oven 45 minutes, or until hot and bubbly.

Old-Fashioned Lasagna

Christine W. Randall
Assistant Features Editor, *The Post and Courier*, Charleston, SC

I grew up on my mother's lasagna, which spoiled me for most others. Over the years I have adapted the recipe a little. For example, she cooks her lasagna noodles beforehand. I find that too messy and time consuming, so I adjust the cooking time and use uncooked noodles.

Makes 8 servings

2 tablespoons vegetable oil
1/2 cup finely chopped onions
1 pound lean ground beef
2 1/2 cups chopped tomatoes
1 (8-ounce) can tomato sauce
8 tablespoons grated Parmesan cheese, divided
3 tablespoons chopped fresh parsley

2 cloves garlic, finely chopped
1 1/2 teaspoons salt
1/4 teaspoon black pepper
1/4 teaspoon dried oregano
6 (1 1/2-inch wide) lasagna noodles
12 ounces mozzarella cheese, sliced
1 (16-ounce) carton cottage cheese

The day before or early in the day: Heat oil in a large skillet. Add onions; cook, stirring, until tender. Add beef; cook, stirring, until brown. Add tomatoes, tomato sauce, 2 tablespoons of the Parmesan cheese, parsley, garlic, salt, pepper and oregano. Simmer, covered, 30 minutes. Refrigerate until ready to assemble lasagna.

About an hour before serving time: Spread one-third of the meat sauce in a 13x9x2-inch baking pan. Place 3 uncooked lasagna noodles on the sauce. Top with half of the mozzarella cheese and half of the cottage cheese. Repeat layers, ending with sauce. Top with the remaining 6 tablespoons Parmesan cheese.

Cover pan with aluminum foil. Bake in a preheated 350° oven 30 minutes. Remove foil, and bake 15 minutes, or until hot and bubbly. Let stand 20 minutes before serving.

6 ounces of pure alcohol is equal to about 12 bottles of beer or 8 mixed drinks.

Pasta a la Cairo

Jim Hillibish
City Editor, *The Repository*, Canton, OH

This delicate but filling pasta main dish is enjoyed in the alley restaurants of Cairo, where it is served on huge platters ringed with sliced lemons and lettuce greens. The sauce should have a custard texture, so be careful not to overcook it.

Makes 6 to 8 servings

16 ounces large elbow macaroni (4 cups)	1/4 cup all-purpose flour
	1 cup milk
3 tablespoons butter, divided	4 eggs, divided
1 medium onion, thinly sliced	2 cups chicken broth
1 pound ground lamb	1/2 teaspoon ground nutmeg
Salt and black pepper	1/2 teaspoon ground ginger

Cook macaroni according to package directions. Drain well.

Melt 1 tablespoon of the butter in a large skillet. Add onion; cook, stirring, until onion is tender. Add lamb; cook, stirring, 12 to 15 minutes, or until brown. Season to taste with salt and pepper.

Melt remaining 2 tablespoons butter in a saucepan. Remove from heat. Stir in flour, mixing well. In another saucepan, combine milk and 3 eggs; beat well with a fork. Heat mixture over low heat. Slowly whisk warm milk mixture into flour mixture, mixing well. Add broth, nutmeg and ginger; mix well. Cook over low heat, stirring constantly, until mixture is thick.

Add half of the sauce to cooked macaroni; mix gently. Spoon half of macaroni mixture into a lightly greased 13x9x2-inch baking pan. Spread lamb mixture over macaroni mixture. Top lamb with remaining macaroni mixture. Pour the remaining sauce over all.

Beat the remaining 1 egg; spread beaten egg over the top of the casserole.

Bake, uncovered, in a preheated 350° oven 30 minutes, or until hot and bubbly. Check occasionally; the sauce should cook to a custard-like texture. Let stand 10 minutes before serving to allow flavors to meld.

Spaghetti with Beef and Mushrooms

Jeanne Voltz
Cookbook Author, Pittsboro, NC

My husband remembered "spaghetti and daube" (pronounced dobe) that he had as a child growing up in New Orleans. I studied recipes for the country French stew called daube, thinking the Creole sauce was adapted from the French. This is a far cry from the ancient daube and probably holds little resemblance to my husband's memory food, but it is a good change from spaghetti and tomato sauce.

Makes 4 to 6 servings

1 teaspoon vegetable oil
2 ounces smoked bacon, cut into small pieces
1 beef top round steak (1 to 1 1/2 pounds)
1 medium onion, chopped
2 cloves garlic, finely chopped
1/4 cup finely chopped fresh parsley
1 bay leaf
1 white turnip or parsnip, chopped

3 carrots, cut into chunks
1 to 2 dried hot chili peppers
1 1/2 to 2 cups beef broth, divided
1 teaspoon salt, or to taste
1/4 teaspoon freshly ground black pepper
2 teaspoons butter
6 to 8 ounces fresh mushrooms, sliced
1 to 1 1/2 pounds thin spaghetti

Heat oil in a Dutch oven. Add bacon; cook and stir 3 to 4 minutes. Add beef; brown on both sides. Stir in onion and garlic; cook 1 to 2 minutes. Stir in parsley, bay leaf, turnip, carrots, chili pepper, 1/2 cup of the beef broth, salt and pepper. Place a sheet of foil or waxed paper over the pan and cover tightly with the lid to hold in steam. Simmer at the lowest heat possible for 2 to 3 hours, or until the meat falls apart in shreds when poked with a fork. Every 30 minutes, stir mixture and add more beef broth if needed to keep meat moist but not floating; reseal the pan.

Remove the meat from the sauce and shred it. Return shredded meat to sauce. Remove and discard bay leaf and chili pepper.

Melt butter in a skillet. Add mushrooms and cook, stirring, until juices evaporate. Stir mushrooms into meat sauce.

Drunk driving is the most frequently committed violent crime in America.

Cook spaghetti according to package directions. Drain. Mix the hot cooked spaghetti with the meat sauce. Serve immediately.

Note: The meat and sauce can be cooked the day before, refrigerated and reheated with the mushrooms just before serving with the spaghetti.

Straw and Hay

Eleanor Ostman
Food Writer, *St. Paul Pioneer Press*, St. Paul, MN

This two-tone Italian pasta has been a classic at our house for so long its source has drifted from my memory. I know it became part of our repertoire about the time that America discovered pasta with white sauces, but before the time we all started counting fat grams. In a household where new recipes are always being tested and old ones seldom get a reprise, this is one that has been resurrected time and again for quick entertaining.

Makes 4 to 6 servings

16 ounces fresh or dried linguine (half plain, half spinach)
1 clove garlic, cut in half
1/4 cup butter
8 ounces fresh mushrooms, sliced
1 1/2 cups cooked ham cut into thin strips
1 cup heavy cream
1/2 cup half-and-half or light cream
1 cup fresh or frozen green peas
Freshly grated nutmeg
White pepper
Freshly grated Parmesan or Asiago cheese

Cook pasta according to package directions. Drain well.

Meanwhile, rub a large skillet with a cut piece of garlic; discard garlic. Melt butter in skillet. Add mushrooms; cook, stirring, until light brown. Stir in ham, cream, half-and-half and peas. Cook, stirring occasionally, until sauce is reduced by about one third. Season to taste with nutmeg and white pepper.

Add pasta to sauce. Toss lightly with two forks, sprinkling with cheese while mixing. Pass additional cheese at the table.

Sunshine Stir-Fry

Janet Geissler
Food Editor, *Lansing State Journal*, Lansing, MI

When we think of pasta, the first nationality that usually comes to mind is Italian. But many Asian dishes call for noodles. This Asian-inspired dish is light and flavorful. It combines the sweetness of pineapple with the tang of green bell pepper.

Makes 4 servings

4 ounces spaghetti
1 (20-ounce) can pineapple chunks
1 whole chicken breast, skinned
    and boned
2 tablespoons vegetable oil
2 large cloves garlic, pressed
2 tablespoons finely chopped fresh
    ginger or 1 teaspoon
    ground ginger

2 medium carrots, sliced
1 green bell pepper, cut into strips
1/3 cup soy sauce
1 tablespoon cornstarch
1 tablespoon sesame oil
3 green onions, sliced

Cook spaghetti according to package directions. Drain.

Drain pineapple, reserving 1/3 cup juice.

Cut chicken into bite-size chunks. Heat oil in a large skillet. Add chicken, garlic and ginger. Cook, stirring, over high heat 2 minutes. Add drained pineapple, carrots and bell pepper. Cover; steam 2 to 3 minutes, or until vegetables are tender-crisp. Stir in cooked spaghetti.

In a small bowl, combine reserved 1/3 cup pineapple juice, soy sauce, cornstarch and sesame oil; mix well. Pour over chicken mixture. Add green onions. Cook, stirring, until sauce is slightly thickened and ingredients are heated through. Serve immediately.

Intoxication rates for drivers in fatal crashes were highest for motorcyclists.

Third-Best Spaghetti Sauce

Eleanor Ostman
Food Writer, *St. Paul Pioneer Press*, St. Paul, MN

Until computers and pagination took over, newspapers had large and boisterous composing rooms where type was set and pages were "composed," or laid out, prior to printing. The composing room was largely a male, macho domain, but several of the guys liked to talk about their cooking prowess. One of them shared what he called Second-Best Spaghetti Sauce. I was never quite sure what was "first best." After that recipe ran in the food section, a reader, Audrey Ferrey of Shoreview, Minn., countered by sending in Third-Best Spaghetti Sauce. Her slightly sweet, well-balanced sauce was much less complicated to make than Second Best. For that, I liked it a lot.

Makes about 6 cups; enough for 4 servings of pasta

3 tablespoons vegetable oil
2 cloves garlic
1 pound lean ground beef
1 large onion, finely chopped
2 tablespoons all-purpose flour
1 (15-ounce) can tomatoes, undrained
2 (6-ounce) cans tomato paste

3/4 cup water
1 tablespoon granulated sugar
2 teaspoons salt
1 teaspoon Worcestershire sauce
1/2 teaspoon black pepper
1/2 teaspoon garlic powder
Dash hot pepper sauce
Hot cooked pasta

Heat oil in a large skillet. Add whole garlic cloves; cook, stirring, 1 minute. Remove and discard garlic. Add beef and onion to skillet; cook, stirring, until meat is brown. Add flour to meat mixture; mix well. Add tomatoes with their liquid, tomato paste, water, sugar, salt, Worcestershire sauce, pepper, garlic powder and hot pepper sauce; mix well. Simmer about 1 hour, stirring occasionally. The sauce will be thick; it can be thinned, if desired, with water or tomato juice.

Serve sauce over your choice of hot cooked pasta.

Turkey Tetrazzini

Leona Carlson
Food Writer (Retired), *Rockford Register Star*, Rockford, IL

Leftover turkey never tasted better — nor did it the first time around for that matter — than in this dish. It's my favorite recipe for post-holiday leftovers. It's not only tasty, but also easy to prepare. It can be assembled ahead of time and refrigerated or frozen until baking time. It goes well with leftover accompaniments such as cranberry or raspberry molded salads.

Makes 6 servings

1/4 cup butter or margarine
3/4 pound fresh mushrooms, sliced
1/2 small green bell pepper, cut into strips
3 tablespoons all-purpose flour
2 teaspoons salt
1/4 teaspoon black pepper
2 1/2 cups light cream or half-and-half

4 cups chopped cooked turkey
2 pimentos, drained and chopped
1/4 cup frozen cholesterol-free real egg product, thawed and slightly beaten
6 ounces thin spaghetti
Grated Parmesan cheese

Melt butter in a medium saucepan. Add mushrooms and bell pepper; cook 5 minutes. Stir in flour, salt and pepper. Gradually stir in cream; mix well. Cook over low heat, stirring frequently, until sauce thickens. Stir in turkey and pimentos; cook until heated through. Remove from heat. Combine turkey mixture with egg product; mix well.

Meanwhile, cook spaghetti according to package directions. Drain well. Put spaghetti in a greased 12x8x2-inch baking pan. Pour turkey mixture over spaghetti; sprinkle cheese on top. Bake in a preheated 300° oven 45 to 50 minutes, or until hot and bubbly.

Note: Cholesterol-watchers can substitute skim milk for the cream and omit the cheese topping. Use nonstick vegetable cooking spray instead of butter to grease the pan, if desired.

A .02 BAC can affect driving abilities and increase the chances of a crash.

Gnocchi, Couscous, Dumplings, Etc.

Cold Noodles with Sesame Sauce

Kasey Wilson
Food Columnist, *The Vancouver Courier*, Vancouver, BC, Canada

Treat your friends to one of my favorite starters for a Chinese dinner. The recipe comes from my friend Tony Vong, of the popular Vong's Kitchen in Vancouver. All of the ingredients can be obtained at Chinese or Asian food stores. This sesame sauce keeps two weeks in the refrigerator or several months in the freezer. The sauce also is good heated and served as a dipping sauce with stir-fried chicken or meat.

Makes 4 servings

3 tablespoons peanut oil or
  vegetable oil
4 medium cloves garlic,
  finely chopped
6 tablespoons sesame seed paste or
  unsalted smooth peanut butter
1/2 teaspoon chopped dried red
  chili pepper

3 tablespoons granulated sugar
2 tablespoons dark soy sauce
1 1/2 teaspoons salt
16 ounces Chinese egg noodles
4 ounces thinly sliced barbecued
  pork or chicken
1 cup fresh bean sprouts,
  rinsed and drained

Set a wok or skillet over high heat for 30 seconds. Add oil; heat 30 seconds. Add garlic, sesame seed paste and chili pepper; mix well. Add sugar, soy sauce and salt; mix well. Remove sauce from wok and let cool. You should have about 1 cup sesame sauce.

Cook noodles according to package directions. Pour into a colander to drain. Rinse with cold water; drain again.

Put the cold noodles in a bowl. Add 1/3 cup of the sesame sauce; mix well. Arrange seasoned noodles on a platter; scatter barbecued pork and bean sprouts on top. Serve cold.

Refrigerate remaining sesame sauce for future use.

The risk of a crash increases greatly at a .05 blood alcohol content.

Couscous and Shrimp Salad

Caroline Stuart
Cookbook Author, Greenwich, CT

Couscous is a staple of North African cooking, and is becoming popular elsewhere. It is now readily available in most U.S. supermarkets. This is an uncomplicated dish that is easy enough for teenagers to make. This light salad is perfect for a party buffet or to take to the beach. It can be served as a side dish or main course. Pine nuts add flavor and texture, the pimento adds color.

Makes 4 servings

10 ounces couscous (1 1/2 cups)
1/3 cup sliced green onions
1/4 cup finely chopped canned pimento
1/4 cup finely chopped fresh parsley
1/4 cup pine nuts

12 large shrimp, cooked, peeled and deveined
1/3 cup tarragon vinegar
1/3 cup vegetable oil
Salt and freshly ground black pepper

Cook couscous according to package directions. Stir with a fork to break up any lumps.

In a large bowl, combine cooked couscous, green onions, pimento, parsley and pine nuts; mix well. Add shrimp; mix gently.

In a small bowl, whisk together vinegar and oil. Pour over couscous mixture; mix gently. Season to taste with salt and pepper. Serve warm, at room temperature, or chilled.

Dessert Couscous

Constance Hay
Free-Lance Food Writer, Columbia, MD

Couscous, the tiny pasta of Morocco, has become a welcome addition to the American diet in the past few years. It is found in most supermarkets and is now available in a quick-cooking variety. Don't think couscous is limited to savory main dishes. It's versatile enough to use in desserts, too. You can vary this light dessert by using different fruits depending on the season or substituting your favorite dried fruits during the winter.

Makes 4 servings

1 cup milk
3 1/3 ounces quick-cooking
  couscous (1/2 cup)
1 tablespoon butter or margarine
1/8 teaspoon salt

1/2 cup vanilla yogurt
1/2 cup fresh berries
  (blueberries, raspberries or
  sliced strawberries)

Bring milk just to boiling in a medium saucepan. Gradually add couscous; mix well. Stir in butter and salt. Return to boiling; cook, stirring constantly, 2 minutes, or until milk is absorbed. Remove from heat. Cover and let stand 15 minutes.

Fluff couscous with a fork. Stir in yogurt. Gently fold in berries. Garnish each serving with additional berries, if desired.

No one is safe from people who drive under the influence of alcohol.

Gingery Calamari with Noodles

Anita Stewart
Executive Director, *Cuisine Canada*, Elora, Ontario, Canada

In this recipe, I have married seafood with classic Asian seasonings, including one of my personal favorites, hoisin sauce, which is available in Chinese groceries. If calamari is not available, try tuna, swordfish or shark. They are all firm enough to hold together during stir-frying.

Makes 6 servings

1 pound calamari, cleaned and sliced into 1/2-inch rings
2 tablespoons hoisin sauce
2 tablespoons orange juice
1 tablespoon grated fresh ginger
1 tablespoon soy sauce
2 teaspoons sesame oil, divided
1/2 teaspoon freshly ground black pepper
1/4 to 1/2 teaspoon cayenne pepper, to taste

12 ounces Asian egg noodles
1 tablespoon peanut oil or vegetable oil
1 red bell pepper, cut into strips
1/2 cup chopped peanuts
1 (10-ounce) can sliced water chestnuts, drained
1 to 2 green onions, sliced diagonally

Place calamari in shallow glass pan. Stir together hoisin sauce, orange juice, ginger, soy sauce, 1 teaspoon of the sesame oil, black pepper and cayenne; mix well. Pour marinade over calamari. Refrigerate, covered, 30 minutes, or up to 4 hours.

Cook noodles according to package directions. Drain. Keep warm on a serving platter.

Meanwhile, place wok over high heat. Add remaining 1 teaspoon sesame oil and the peanut oil. Add calamari with its marinade, bell pepper, peanuts and water chestnuts. Stir-fry 2 minutes. Working quickly, pour calamari mixture over cooked noodles; mix gently. Garnish with green onions. Serve immediately.

Note: You can use any very thin egg noodle (similar to angel hair), if you can't find Asian noodles.

Gnocchi Romano

Susan Manlin Katzman
Free-Lance Food Writer, St. Louis, MO

Once upon a time, before butter was banned and heavy cream was criticized, I made a heavenly dish called Gnocchi Romano. I served it at dinner parties, and especially loved gnocchi as a side dish to Steak au Poivre, because the rich farina eased the bite of pepper in the steak. Butter, cream, eggs, cheese and red meat. Sigh! Those were the good old days. I have given up red meat, but I will never abandon Gnocchi Romano. It is just too wonderful to let slip into healthful obscurity.

Makes 6 to 8 servings

3 cups milk
2 tablespoons butter
1 1/2 teaspoons salt
Dash black pepper
Dash ground nutmeg
1 cup uncooked farina
   (cream of wheat)

2 cups heavy cream, divided
3 eggs, beaten
4 to 6 tablespoons butter, melted
3/4 cup finely shredded Swiss
   cheese (3 ounces)

Combine milk, 2 tablespoons butter, salt, pepper and nutmeg in a large saucepan. Bring to boiling. Slowly add farina, stirring vigorously. Simmer, stirring, 3 to 5 minutes, or until mixture is thick.

In a small bowl, combine 1 cup of the cream and eggs; mix well. Stir into farina mixture. Bring mixture to boiling, stirring constantly. Remove from heat.

Lightly grease a 15x10x1-inch baking pan. Spread farina mixture in pan to a thickness of 1/2- to 3/4-inch. Refrigerate several hours, or until mixture is set and chilled.

Put the melted butter in a small bowl. Brush a 10-inch round baking dish or similar size rectangular baking dish with some of the melted butter. With a 1 1/2-inch biscuit cutter, cut circles of farina. Dip each farina circle in the melted butter, then arrange circles overlapping in baking dish. As you cut circles, gather scraps of cold farina and press into circles; dip these in melted butter and add to dish. Sprinkle cheese over farina circles.

Drunk driving deaths have decreased nearly 40% since MADD was founded.

Bake, uncovered, in a preheated 425° oven 10 to 15 minutes, or until cheese melts and mixture is light brown. Pour remaining 1 cup cream over the circles. Return to oven and bake about 10 minutes, or until cream is absorbed and top is golden brown. Let stand 5 minutes before serving.

Great Tomato-Mint Couscous

Caroline Stuart
Cookbook Author, Greenwich, CT

Couscous is actually a type of pasta, made with semolina flour. It is a key ingredient in the foods of North Africa. Couscous makes an interesting side dish or salad and can be combined with vegetables, chicken or lamb.

Makes 4 servings

6 3/4 ounces couscous (1 cup)
3 tablespoons olive oil
5 to 8 fresh plum (Roma) tomatoes
1 cup packed fresh mint leaves,
   stems removed

3 tablespoons white wine vinegar
Salt and freshly ground black
   pepper, to taste

Cook couscous according to package directions. Stir with a fork to break up any lumps. Stir in olive oil. Set aside to cool completely.

Meanwhile, seed tomatoes and chop into ½-inch cubes. Finely chop mint leaves.

In a large bowl, combine cooled couscous, tomatoes, mint, vinegar, salt and pepper; mix gently. Serve immediately, or refrigerate covered until serving time.

Lamb Couscous

Cynthia David
Food Editor, *Toronto Sun*, Toronto, Ontario, Canada

Enjoy the exotic flavors and vibrant colors of the Middle East in this lamb stir-fry served over couscous. Refrigerate or freeze the meat until firm, then cut it thin to make quick-cooking slices. This is one of those recipes that can be tailored to taste. If you're not keen on currants, leave them out. If pine nuts will blow your budget, ignore them. You'll still have an exciting blend of flavors and textures.

Makes 4 servings

4 1/2 ounces quick-cooking couscous (2/3 cup)
1/3 dried currants
1/2 cup chicken broth, heated to boiling
3 tablespoons olive oil
12 ounces lean boneless lamb, cut into thin slices
3 cloves garlic, finely chopped
3 medium carrots, thinly sliced

1 large tart apple, chopped
1 medium-size red bell pepper, cut into 1/2-inch cubes
4 green onions, finely chopped
1/4 cup pine nuts
2 teaspoons lemon juice
1 teaspoon ground cinnamon
1/2 teaspoon cayenne pepper
Salt and black pepper, to taste

Place couscous and currants in a bowl. Pour boiling broth over mixture. Stir with a fork. Cover bowl and set aside 5 minutes, or until liquid is absorbed.

Heat olive oil in a large heavy skillet over high heat. Add lamb and garlic. Stir-fry briefly, then reduce heat to medium. Add carrots; cover and cook 4 minutes, or until lamb is no longer pink and carrots are softened.

Fluff couscous with a fork. Add couscous and currants, apple, bell pepper, green onions, pine nuts, lemon juice, cinnamon, cayenne, salt and pepper to lamb mixture in skillet; mix gently. Cook, covered, about 3 minutes, or just until heated through, stirring occasionally. Serve immediately.

In 1994, the impaired driving death toll was approximately 16,589.

Moroccan Couscous with Oranges

Lori Longbotham
Free-Lance Food Writer, New York, NY

Almost no one will dispute that Moroccan food is among the best cuisines in the world. Couscous, Moroccan pasta, is a big part of that cuisine. While couscous can take all day to prepare, it also can be on the table in a matter of minutes, depending on the preparation method. Serve this fancy but quick and easy side dish with even the simplest entree and you will have a special occasion meal in a flash.

Makes 4 servings

2 navel oranges, peeled and segmented
2 tablespoons finely chopped red onion
1/4 teaspoon granulated sugar
Dash ground cinnamon
Dash salt
Dash cayenne pepper
1 cup reduced-sodium chicken broth
2 tablespoons butter
2 (2-inch) strips orange peel (colored part only)

1 bay leaf
1/2 teaspoon salt
1/2 teaspoon ground cumin
1/2 teaspoon ground coriander seeds
1/4 teaspoon cayenne pepper
1/8 teaspoon ground turmeric
6 3/4 ounces quick-cooking couscous (1 cup)
2 tablespoons chopped fresh cilantro, for garnish

In a small bowl, stir together oranges, red onion, sugar, cinnamon, dash salt and dash cayenne; mix well.

In a medium saucepan, combine broth, butter, orange peel, bay leaf, 1/2 teaspoon salt, cumin, coriander, 1/4 teaspoon cayenne and turmeric; bring to boiling. Stir in couscous. Remove pan from heat. Cover and let stand 5 minutes, or until liquid is absorbed. Fluff couscous with a fork. Remove and discard the orange peel and bay leaf.

Arrange cooked couscous mixture on a serving platter; top with orange mixture. Garnish with cilantro. Serve immediately.

Old-Fashioned Chicken and Dumplings

Barbara Gibbs Ostmann
Food Writer, St. Louis, MO

Beulah Gratzer is God's gift to the First United Methodist Church of St. Clair, Mo. Although the church is full of good cooks, Beulah is one of the best. The church's main fund-raising event is the annual chicken and dumpling dinner in November, and Beulah leads the kitchen team. Although she often uses more than 100 chickens and 150 pounds of flour for the church dinner, she has a family-size recipe, too. These aren't the drop dumplings my grandmother used to make. These are called flat, slick, slippery or rolled dumplings, depending on what part of the country you're from. Call them what you will, I call them delicious.

Makes about 8 servings

1 large, fat stewing hen (about 6 pounds)	Dumplings:
	6 cups sifted all-purpose flour
2 ribs celery	3 eggs
1 bay leaf	2 teaspoons baking powder
1 small onion	1 teaspoon salt
1 teaspoon salt	1/2 teaspoon black pepper
Water	2 teaspoons dried parsley

Put hen, celery, bay leaf, onion (whole) and salt in a 6- to 8-quart kettle. Add about 3¹/₂ quarts water. Bring to a boil; simmer until chicken is tender. Remove chicken from broth. Let chicken and broth cool separately until lukewarm.

Remove chicken meat from bone; discard skin and bones. Cut or tear chicken into bite-size pieces; reserve. Strain broth; reserve.

For dumplings: Put flour in a large bowl. Make a well in the center of the flour. Pour 2 cups of the reserved broth, eggs, baking powder, salt and pepper into well. Mix together until flour is stiff enough to roll out like pie dough. You may need to add more broth or more flour. With a floured rolling pin on a floured surface, roll out dough about ¹/₈-inch thick. Cut into strips about 1-inch wide; cut strips into 2-inch lengths.

If necessary, add enough water to remaining reserved broth to make 3 quarts. Heat broth to a rolling boil in a large kettle with a heavy

Every week, nearly 319 people are killed in alcohol-related crashes.

bottom. Add dumplings to boiling broth, one at a time, stretching each piece of dough almost to the breaking point before you drop it in.

After all the dumplings have been added to broth, reduce heat to lowest setting and let mixture simmer about 10 minutes. Add reserved chicken and parsley. Cook on lowest heat about 10 minutes or longer. Watch carefully; the mixture tends to stick. You might need to add more broth or water; mixture will thicken as it sets. It should be mostly dumplings with a little liquid.

Let mixture set, off heat, about 20 minutes; this improves flavor and texture. Ladle onto plate and serve hot.

Perfect Curry Couscous

Narcisse S. Cadgène
Free-Lance Writer, New York, NY

Couscous is semolina flour that has been mixed with water, rubbed into tiny granules, and dried. Although it looks like cracked grain, it's actually closer to specks of pasta. Couscous cooks in no time, demands no attention, costs little, and lends itself to different flavors ranging from sticky sweet to savagely spicy. I don't know why we don't eat it every day.

Makes 4 servings

2 cups water
6 3/4 ounces quick-cooking
   couscous (1 cup)
1/4 cup shredded coconut
2 tablespoons curry powder

1/2 teaspoon salt, or to taste
1/4 teaspoon black pepper,
   or to taste
1 tablespoon butter (optional)

Bring water to boiling in a heavy saucepan. Add couscous, coconut, curry powder, salt and pepper; mix well. Return to boiling. Cover tightly and remove from heat; let stand 10 to 15 minutes. Fluff with a fork. If desired, stir in butter. Serve immediately.

Plum Dumplings

Janet Geissler
Food Editor, *Lansing State Journal*, Lansing, MI

This was my favorite meal prepared by my German grandmother. Even as a small child, I could eat about eight dumplings. Grandma never used a recipe. It was "about this much" flour, until "it feels like this." We feared the recipe would be lost, so my mother watched her make them and put measurements on paper. We always ate these as an entree, but you could serve them for breakfast or dessert.

Makes 10 servings

4 large potatoes, peeled and cut into chunks
1 cup cottage cheese
4 eggs

About 3 cups all-purpose flour
1 teaspoon salt
30 large or 45 small fresh Italian prune plums, unpitted

Cover potatoes with salted water. Bring to boiling; cook until tender. Drain. Put potatoes through a ricer or food mill; you should have about 4 cups potatoes. Let cool on paper towels.

Put cottage cheese through a ricer or food mill.

In a large bowl, combine potatoes, cottage cheese, eggs, flour and salt; mix well. You should have a stiff dough. Add more flour, if necessary.

With well-floured hands, pull off a 2-inch piece of dough (about the size of a golf ball). Roll dough into a ball, then flatten into a circle. Wrap dough around a plum; seal well. Repeat with remaining dough and plums. Flour hands often to prevent dough from sticking.

(At this point, dumplings can be frozen, if desired. Put on baking sheets. Freeze until hard, then transfer to plastic freezer bags. Thaw before cooking.)

To cook, drop dumplings into boiling salted water, a few at a time. After dumplings rise to the surface, simmer for 12 to 15 minutes.

Serve plain, or top with melted butter and a sprinkling of sugar and cinnamon.

Note: Be sure to caution your guests that the pits are in the plums. However, the pits are easily removed with a fork or spoon while eating.

Approximately every 32 minutes, another person dies in an alcohol-related crash.

Pot Stickers

Toni Burks
Free-Lance Writer, Roanoke, VA

Asian dishes require a lot of attention to the details of preparation, but the results are oh-so-good. These dumplings use many of the bits and pieces of ingredients that often accumulate in the refrigerator. They are delightful as an appetizer or first course.

Makes 30

1 tablespoon butter
1 cup shredded fresh spinach or cabbage
1 cup coarsely grated carrots
1 cup chopped fresh bean sprouts
1 green onion, finely chopped
1/4 pound fresh mushrooms, chopped
3/4 cup cooked rice, chilled

2 tablespoons soy sauce
1 tablespoon oyster sauce
2 teaspoons grated fresh ginger
30 wonton wrappers
3 tablespoons vegetable oil
1/3 cup chicken broth
1 teaspoon balsamic vinegar
1 teaspoon honey

Melt butter in a 12-inch skillet. Add spinach, carrots, bean sprouts, green onion and mushrooms. Cook, stirring, over medium heat 3 minutes. Remove from heat. Add rice, soy sauce, oyster sauce and ginger; mix well.

Cut corners from wonton wrappers to make circles if round wrappers are not available. Place 1 heaping tablespoon vegetable mixture in center of each wonton wrapper. Moisten edges of wrapper with water. Fold over to enclose filling. Pinch edges together, pleating slightly.

Heat oil in a 12-inch skillet. Add dumplings. Cook over medium heat about 3 minutes, or until bottoms are golden brown. Reduce heat to low.

In a small bowl, combine chicken broth, vinegar and honey; mix well. Carefully pour into skillet. Cover and cook over low heat 15 to 20 minutes, or until liquid has evaporated. Serve immediately.

Southwestern Ravioli

Teri M. Grimes
Features Editor, *The Bradenton Herald*, Bradenton, FL

I love to make Chinese dumplings using wonton wrappers; it's quick and easy. Imagine my surprise when I realized I could use the wrappers to make ravioli as well. The procedure is pretty much the same, only the fillings are different. This is one of my favorite combinations. It gets its Southwestern flavor from the cumin, corn and peppers. If you don't want to bother making the sauce, just add some chopped cilantro to your favorite tomato sauce; it's almost as good.

Makes 24

Filling:
2 tablespoons butter
1/4 cup finely chopped onion
1 cup fresh or frozen corn kernels
1 (7 1/2-ounce) jar roasted red bell peppers, drained and finely chopped
1/2 teaspoon ground cumin
1 1/4 cups shredded Monterey Jack cheese with peppers (5 ounces)
Salt and black pepper

Sauce:
1/4 cup butter
2 cloves garlic, finely chopped
1 (28-ounce) can plum (Roma) tomatoes, drained and coarsely chopped
2 tablespoons fresh lime juice
1/4 cup finely chopped fresh cilantro
Salt and black pepper

Assembly:
48 wonton wrappers
Fresh cilantro sprigs, for garnish

For filling: Melt butter in a heavy skillet over low heat. Add onion; cook, stirring, until onion is soft but not brown. Add corn; cook 2 minutes, or until corn is tender. Stir in peppers and cumin. Cook, stirring, 2 minutes. Transfer vegetable mixture to a bowl; let cool completely. Stir in cheese. Season to taste with salt and pepper. Refrigerate, covered, 1 hour, or until well chilled.

Every two minutes, a person is injured in an alcohol-related crash.

For sauce: Melt butter in a large skillet. Add garlic; cook over low heat, stirring, 1 minute. Stir in tomatoes. Bring to boiling over medium-high heat. Simmer, stirring, 10 minutes, or until mixture thickens. Stir in lime juice and cilantro. Season to taste with salt and pepper. Cover and keep warm while preparing ravioli.

To assemble ravioli: Place 1 wonton wrapper on a lightly floured surface. Mound 1 tablespoon chilled vegetable mixture in the center of the wrapper. Moisten edges of wrapper with water. Put a second wrapper over filled one, pressing down around the filling to force out air and seal edges. If desired, trim the excess dough around the filling with a knife or decorative cutter. Repeat with remaining wrappers and vegetable filling, to make 24 ravioli. Put ravioli on a dry, clean kitchen towel; turn them occasionally so they will dry on all sides.

To cook ravioli: Bring a large pot of salted water to boiling. Add ravioli, a few at a time. Cook about 2 minutes, or until they rise to the surface and are tender. Do not crowd them in the pot. Transfer cooked ravioli with a slotted spoon to paper towels to drain. Keep warm while cooking the remaining ravioli.

To serve: Spoon some sauce onto each of 8 heated serving plates. Arrange 3 ravioli on each plate. Garnish with fresh cilantro, if desired. Serve hot.

Summer Squash Couscous

Carolyn Flournoy
Food Columnist, *The Times*, Shreveport, LA

A Lebanese friend introduced me to the glories of couscous, and I have been designing dishes using it ever since. In our part of the country, the crop of summer squash—both yellow crookneck and zucchini—is at times overwhelming, so I am always looking for ways to use it. Squash couscous can be served hot, or you can refrigerate it, pack it in a cooler and take it to a picnic.

Makes 4 servings

6 3/4 ounces couscous (1 cup)
1 tablespoon vegetable oil
1 tablespoon olive oil (preferably extra virgin)
2/3 cup coarsely chopped yellow squash
2/3 cup chopped zucchini
1/2 cup chopped onion
1/2 teaspoon finely chopped garlic
1 cup cooked or canned garbanzo beans, drained
1/2 teaspoon ground cumin
1/2 teaspoon crushed red pepper
Salt and seasoned pepper, to taste
1/3 cup chopped fresh parsley

Cook couscous according to package directions. Fluff with a fork. (You need about 3 cups cooked couscous for this recipe.)

Meanwhile, heat vegetable oil and olive oil in a large saucepan. Add yellow squash, zucchini, onion and garlic; cook, stirring, about 4 minutes, or until tender. Stir in garbanzos, cumin, red pepper flakes, salt and seasoned pepper. Add cooked couscous, stirring gently. Cook 6 to 8 minutes, or until heated through. Transfer to a serving bowl and garnish with parsley. Serve hot, or, refrigerate, covered, and serve chilled.

34 fewer people die in alcohol-related crashes every day since MADD began.

Sweet Couscous

Barbara Gibbs Ostmann
Food Writer, St. Louis, MO

On a study tour of Morocco with Oldways Preservation and Exchange Trust, a Boston-based food think tank, I learned more about couscous in a few days than I had known in my entire life. As shown by other recipes in this chapter, couscous is a versatile dish. Although it is usually savory, sweet couscous, or seffa, is also popular, especially with children. This recipe is adapted from one by Kitty Morse, an expert on Moroccan cuisine and author of several cookbooks.

Makes 10 servings

16 ounces couscous (2 1/4 cups)
1/2 cup golden raisins
1 cup butter or margarine, divided
1/4 cup whole or slivered almonds
1/4 cup granulated sugar

1 tablespoon ground cinnamon
1/4 cup orange blossom water (available in specialty food shops)
Additional granulated sugar and ground cinnamon, for serving

Prepare couscous as directed on package, using water instead of broth. You can use either regular or quick-cooking couscous.

While couscous is cooking, cover raisins with hot water and let soak. Drain well before using.

Melt 2 tablespoons of the butter in a skillet. Add almonds; cook, stirring, 2 minutes, or until light brown.

When couscous is cooked, fluff with a fork to break up any lumps. Add remaining 14 tablespoons butter; stir until butter melts. Stir in sugar, cinnamon and orange blossom water.

Heap the couscous on a serving platter. Garnish with almonds and drained raisins. Put the platter in the middle of the table. Put a small bowl of sugar and a small bowl of cinnamon alongside, so guests can sweeten the couscous to taste. Serve for dessert with a glass of milk or buttermilk.

Swiss Dumplings with Sauerkraut

Barbara Gibbs Ostmann
Food Writer, St. Louis, MO

Switzerland is my adopted country. After living there for three years in the early '70s, I try to return as often as possible to visit friends, hike along scenic mountain paths and sample regional specialties. Erika Faisst Lieben, of Switzerland Tourism, is a terrific cook, and together we're working on a Swiss cookbook. This recipe for Suurchruutknoepfli is adapted from one in her personal collection. It's perfect for a hearty dinner after a day of winter sports. Dumplings are especially popular in the German-speaking areas of Switzerland.

Makes 6 servings

About 3½ cups unsifted all-purpose flour
2 teaspoons salt
4 eggs
½ cup (or more) milk
1 (16-ounce) package sauerkraut
½ cup butter, divided
3 yellow onions, thinly sliced, divided

8 juniper berries
1 teaspoon caraway seeds (optional)
1 bay leaf
1 cup water or broth
1 smoked pig's knuckle, cooked in water to cover until very tender (meat should fall off bone)

Sift flour into a large bowl; make a well in the center. Add salt and eggs to well. Stir with a fork, incorporating more and more flour and adding milk whenever dough gets too dry. When flour and milk are incorporated, the dough should be very soft and thick. Using a wooden spoon, beat the dough in the bowl, working from one side to the other; beat hard, going deeply into the dough. Blisters will immediately form on the surface of the dough. Let dough rest for 30 minutes.

Rinse sauerkraut under cold water; drain well.

Melt ¼ cup of the butter in a large, non-reactive skillet. Add one-third of the onion slices; cook until soft and light brown. Add drained sauerkraut and mix well to coat with butter; cook 5 minutes. Add juniper berries, caraway seeds, bay leaf and water. Cover and cook over medium heat, stirring occasionally, 1½ hours, or until very soft; be careful not to let mixture burn on bottom. Add a little water or broth if mixture gets too dry.

Meanwhile, remove meat from bone of cooked pig's knuckle; shred meat. Add shredded pork to sauerkraut mixture during last 10 minutes of cooking time.

About 30 minutes before sauerkraut mixture is done, bring a large pot of salted water to a rolling boil. Ladle $1/2$ cup Knoepfli (dumpling) dough onto a small, thin wooden board. With a knife, scrape small slivers of dough into the boiling water. When Knoepfli rise to the surface, lift them out with a slotted spoon, refresh under cold water and drain well. Continue until all dough is used, being sure to bring water to a full boil each time before adding dough; replenish water in pot, if necessary.

Warm a deep serving platter. Put a layer of Knoepfli in platter and top with a layer of sauerkraut mixture; repeat layers, ending with a layer of Knoepfli.

Melt the remaining $1/4$ cup butter in a small skillet; add the remaining two-thirds of the onion slices and fry until crisp and brown. Pour onions and butter over Knoepfli; serve immediately.

Thai Sautéed Noodles

Lori Longbotham
Free-Lance Food Writer, New York, NY

This is a great dish for a party. Serve it with grilled chicken or fish for a festive meal. This basic Thai recipe is a study in contrasts – hot, sour, salty and sweet all in one dish. There is another element you can always count on with Thai food – a beautiful appearance.

Makes 8 servings

16 ounces rice noodles (1/8-inch thick) or fine egg noodles
1/2 cup vegetable oil
6 cloves garlic, finely chopped
8 ounces cooked and peeled shrimp, chopped
6 ounces pork tenderloin, trimmed, sliced and chopped
3 eggs, lightly beaten
1/4 cup Thai fish sauce (nam pla)
2 tablespoons light brown sugar

3/4 cup unsweetened canned coconut milk, stirred well
1 1/2 cups chopped dry-roasted peanuts
1 fresh red chili pepper, seeded and finely chopped (or to taste)
6 green onions, finely chopped
1/2 cup finely chopped fresh cilantro
1 lime, thinly sliced crosswise and coarsely chopped

Soak rice noodles in hot water to cover 10 minutes. Drain thoroughly. (If using egg noodles, cook them *al dente* according to package directions. Drain.)

Meanwhile, heat oil in a large skillet or wok over medium-high heat. Add garlic; cook, stirring, until golden.

Put shrimp and pork in food processor or blender; process or blend until coarsely ground. Add to garlic in skillet. Cook, stirring, 4 minutes, or until pork is cooked through. Add eggs; cook just until set. Add fish sauce and brown sugar; stir until sugar dissolves. Add rice noodles (or egg noodles) and coconut milk. Cook, stirring, about 3 minutes, or until noodles are hot.

Transfer mixture to a large platter. Sprinkle with peanuts, chili pepper, green onions, cilantro and lime. Serve immediately.

There are an estimated 2.2 million alcohol-related crashes each year.

Toasted Ravioli

Barbara Gibbs Ostmann
Food Writer, St. Louis, MO

Toasted Ravioli is a St. Louis specialty. According to local newspaper files, the toasted ravioli was created in the late 1930s by happy accident in an Italian restaurant called Oldani's. Legend has it that the cook accidentally dropped a boiled ravioli into hot grease. When it came to the top, he dropped in a few more, then sent a plateful to the bar. The customers loved them and ordered more. The Toasted Ravioli was born. The recipe has evolved over the years, and today's version is usually breaded and served with a tomato or meat sauce.

Makes about 4 servings

2 tablespoons milk
1 egg
1 (1-pound) package frozen ravioli (meat or cheese filled), thawed
2/3 to 1 cup fine dry seasoned bread crumbs

Vegetable oil or shortening, for frying
1 cup spaghetti sauce or pizza sauce
Grated Parmesan cheese

In a small bowl, combine milk and egg; beat well. Dip each ravioli in egg mixture; coat with bread crumbs.

Pour oil to a depth of 2 inches in a heavy 3-quart saucepan. Heat oil to 350°. Carefully add ravioli to hot oil, a few at a time, and cook 1 minute per side, or until golden. Remove with slotted spoon and drain on paper towels. Keep warm in a 300° oven while frying the remaining ravioli.

Meanwhile, heat sauce in a small saucepan. Sprinkle Parmesan cheese over ravioli. Serve ravioli with a bowl of warm sauce for dipping.

Walnut Ravioli

Kasey Wilson
Food Columnist, *The Vancouver Courier*, Vancouver, BC, Canada

If you think making ravioli is a laborious task, you will be delighted at how quickly these pasta packages go together when you use wonton wrappers. These thin egg-noodle wrappers are available in Asian markets and in supermarket produce sections. Wonton wrappers can be kept tightly sealed in the refrigerator for about two weeks.

Makes 12

1/2 cup ricotta cheese
1/2 cup crumbled Gorgonzola cheese
1/4 teaspoon freshly ground black pepper
1/3 cup plus 2 tablespoons chopped walnuts, toasted, divided

24 wonton wrappers
1/2 cup butter
1/2 cup grated Parmesan cheese
Chopped fresh basil, for garnish

For filling, combine ricotta cheese, Gorgonzola cheese, pepper and 2 tablespoons of the walnuts; mix well.

To assemble ravioli, put 2 generous teaspoons of cheese filling in the center of each of 12 wonton wrappers. Moisten edges of wrappers with water. Top each filled wrapper with another wrapper; press to seal edges. Cover with plastic wrap or a damp tea towel so they won't dry out.

Meanwhile, bring a large pot of salted water to boiling. Add ravioli, a few at a time. Cook 2 to 3 minutes, or until ravioli rise to the surface. Remove carefully with a slotted spoon and drain well. Place 3 ravioli on each serving plate; keep warm while cooking remaining ravioli.

Melt butter in a saucepan. Add remaining 1/3 cup walnuts and heat through. Spoon butter and walnuts over each serving, then sprinkle with Parmesan cheese and basil. Serve hot.

Note: To toast walnuts, spread walnuts in an ungreased pan. Bake in a preheated 350° oven 5 to 7 minutes, stirring occasionally, or until brown.

In 1994, about 56% of all drivers involved in fatal crashes were drunk.